WHERE HAVE ALL
THE
EMAILS
GONE?

Dan and Kat

Enjoy

2/09

Other resources from ZATZ Publishing

OutlookPower Magazine (at *OutlookPower.com*) is our general email publication covering Outlook (the email client) and Exchange (the server). Because it covers both sides, we get readers ranging from basic mail users up through enterprise IT staff. There are a few key common denominators among all our readers, the most measurable being that these folks are *intense* email users.

DominoPower Magazine (at *DominoPower.com*) is our Lotus publication and is all about Lotus messaging and collaboration. It's read by virtually all the Lotus network managers, systems engineers, developers, business partners, and key Lotus and IBM personnel.

Computing Unplugged (at *ComputingUnplugged.com*) covers, quite literally, unplugged computing. It covers handheld computers, WiFi, GPS devices, laptops, wireless and cell phone issues, and even robotics. Like *OutlookPower*, coverage and readership range from general consumer coverage through enterprise solutions.

Connected Photographer (at *ConnectedPhotographer.com*) is all about doing cool things with your photographs. We cover everything from studio technique to Photoshop plug-ins, to taking eBay and personals pictures, to cameras, gadgets, sharing, and even cameras in phones, PDAs, and more. This definitely ain't your Daddy's gearhead camera reviews mag!

WebSpherePower Magazine (at *WebSpherePower.com*) provides news and information about IBM's WebSphere initiatives, the open-source Eclipse system, and enterprise Java development.

Resources for this book can be found online at *EmailsGone.com*. Questions and comments on *Where Have All The Emails Gone?* may be sent to:

David Gewirtz
ZATZ Publishing
Email: *david@ZATZ.com*
Web: *ZATZ.com*
Phone: 321-722-4620

WHERE HAVE ALL THE EMAILS GONE?

David Gewirtz

Palm Bay • Florida

Published by ZATZ Publishing, an imprint of Component Enterprises, Inc.
PO Box 110579, Palm Bay, Florida 32911 • (321) 722-4620 • (321) 406-1001 FAX

Printed in the United States of America
Library of Congress Control Number: 2007937415
ISBN (10-digit):   0-945266-20-0
ISBN (13-digit):   978-0-945266-20-4

About the author

David Gewirtz has written more than 600 articles about email, collaboration, and mobile technology. He is the Publisher and Editor-in-Chief of ZATZ Publishing, an independent digital magazine and book publisher.

David is a former professor of computer science, has lectured at Princeton, Berkeley, UCLA, and Stanford, and has been awarded the prestigious Sigma Xi Research Award in Engineering. He is the author of four books including *Where Have All The Emails Gone?* and *The Flexible Enterprise.*

Earlier in his career, he held the unusual title of "Godfather" at Apple, was an executive at Symantec, and served on the board of the Software Entrepreneurs Forum (now SDForum) in the heart of Silicon Valley.

David is the creator of ZENPRESS, a breakthrough technology for Internet magazine production. He is also the lead developer of the MySQL and SQLite database extensions for the open-source Frontier Kernel project and has designed embedded database technology used by more than 2,000 companies, universities, and government agencies.

An accomplished author and photographer, David is also an entertaining and electrifying speaker. His commentaries on technology, industry, and emerging nations have been broadcast into more than 40 countries (all in their own unique translations) by Radio Free Europe and Radio Liberty.

Weaving a tapestry of art, industry, politics, and technology, he brings a unique and powerful perspective to all his audiences. Known for their clarity and insight, his articles reach nearly a million people worldwide each week.

This book is dedicated to the
Constitution of the United States of America.

In other times and in other places, books like this might be banned, burned,
or never published, and the authors captured, killed — or worse.

Because of the U.S. Constitution,
authors like me can tell important stories
to readers like you — and together we can continue to
make our country better, safer, and stronger.

For Secret Service, Congressional investigators, and White House staff

I know you're busy, so here's a quick cheat-sheet:

- If you take anything at all away from this book, let it be this: email in the White House needs to be fixed. It's not just about politics. It's about security.

- For a quick understanding of the root causes and what you can do to fix them, read Chapter 11, "Understanding the root causes" and Chapter 12, "Our final recommendations."

- If you want the hairs on the back of your neck to stand up, if you want to get all freaked out, or if you're with the Secret Service, you'll want to read Chapter 1, "Prepare to be freaked out" and then Chapter 7, "The nightmare scenario."

- If you think this is just a rant on the George W. Bush administration, you're mistaken and you should read Chapter 2, "A historical perspective."

- And, if you think email messages can't just disappear, read Chapter 3, "Can email just disappear?"

Of course, if you really want to understand this issue thoroughly, read the whole book. It's a heck of a story.

Tips from the ZATZ magazines

Wireless security is a real concern, even if all you're running is a small, home network. Open wireless access points can give bad guys access to your personal and financial data, as well as turn your computer into a 'bot, joining millions of other "zombie" machines wreaking havoc on the Internet.

To learn how you can secure your network, read *Computing Unplugged Magazine's* "Please stop clicking on the monkey: a Q&A on home networking security" at *http:// www.computingunplugged.com/issues/ issue200507/00001553001.html.*

Table of Contents

Tips from the ZATZ magazines

The Federal Trade Commission estimates that as many as nine million Americans have their identities stolen each year.

To learn how you can safeguard yourself from identity theft, read *Computing Unplugged Magazine's* "How to protect yourself from identity theft" at *http://www.computingunplugged.com/ issues/issue200601/00001707001.html.*

OutlookPower Magazine also has an excellent article on this topic. Read "Learn more about privacy, identity theft, and anonymous browsing" at *http://www.outlookpower.com/issues/ issue200510/00001650001.html.*

Introduction

Here, there be dragons.

When I started this project, I had no idea what I was getting myself into. I thought I was writing just another little filler article on email to meet my next publishing deadline.

I had no idea I was going to uncover freaky national security problems within the core of White House operations. I had no idea I would find dragons.

I never expected to find a security hole so big you could drive the Capitol Building through it without denting the rotunda.

Don't get me wrong. I've always figured every White House operated a little like a drunken sailor. I just had this little fantasy that a strong desire for self-preservation would motivate the folks working there to self-correct from their dumber impulses.

Apparently, I was wrong. At least as far as internal email operations go, the White House apparently operates like a stupid drunken sailor on crack. As any seasoned Chief Petty Officer knows, stupid drunken sailors on crack can get themselves into all sorts of trouble. The White House isn't much different.

Let me give you a little background before I tell you more about that.

Politics as spectator sport

I minored in ethics and political philosophy. It's the political philosophy part of my minor that generally made me annoying to my friends. It was the ethics part that made me annoying to my employers. Go figure.

Politics is my spectator sport. Much as Chicago Cubs fans have long had a morbid fascination with the Cubbies, I've long had a morbid fascination with the constant pitching and fielding done by the Democrats and the Republicans.

> ## There was really no way to know there was a nightmare scenario hidden inside the incredibly mundane topic that is email.

Just so you know, I've voted for both Democrats and Republicans. I voted for Ronald Reagan, George Herbert Walker Bush, and Bill Clinton. At various times in my life, I've called myself a Republican and at other times, a Democrat. These days, both parties have sufficiently pissed me off that I'm pretty much an independent.

Really, though, I'm a techie. I have a formal honors engineering degree in Computer Science. I got it back in the days when majoring in Computer Science meant something, not like the C.S. degrees kids these days get after they show they can create a Web page.

My day job is as co-founder and Editor-in-Chief of ZATZ Publishing. We publish five technical magazines on the Internet and reach about a million readers a month.

That means I have to kick out a stack of articles each month on topics ranging from email to photography to home entertainment to enterprise security. We publish technology news every day. Four times a month, I've got to come up with fascinating and helpful articles — or at least articles readers will read.

It was meeting that editorial obligation that got me into this mess.

Sticking my nose into the White House's email

Back in April of 2007, it came to America's attention that some email messages from the White House had gone missing. As the publisher of two of the largest publications dedicated to email and electronic communication, *OutlookPower Magazine* and *DominoPower Magazine,* it seemed appropriate for us to investigate this issue.

I honestly expected to write one short article that would discuss the basics of the issue and then forget all about it. Of course, from the news reports in the mainstream media, there was really no way to know there was a nightmare scenario hidden inside the incredibly mundane topic that is email.

Looking at the problem through the eyes of an email expert, I quickly saw some things that both the mainstream media and the Congressional investigators didn't.

Let's start by understanding exactly what the fuss was about. Back then, Karl Rove was Deputy White House Chief of Staff to U.S. President George W. Bush. As part of the ongoing (and highly political) investigation into the firing of eight United States Attorneys, it was discovered that many email messages sent by Mr. Rove allegedly had not been archived — and therefore couldn't be examined for the purposes of the investigation.

It's now come out that there's possibly five million or more email messages missing, and they may include email messages missing from government servers in addition to email messages missing from servers operated by the Republican National Committee.

Looking at the problem through the eyes of an email expert, I quickly saw some things that both the mainstream media and the Congressional investigators didn't.

Just a quick scan of the White House press briefing transcripts uncovered serious concerns about unsecured email communications that might affect national security, transitions in server technology during a time of war that might have caused both communications interruptions and historical records loss, and data management practices that seriously question the technical email infrastructure being used by the Executive Office of the President.

It was time to get serious.

The fact is, if I am to take my job seriously here at ZATZ, there is no topic more appropriate for me to cover. It should be somewhat immodestly noted that because I publish the leading publications for both Microsoft Outlook and IBM Lotus Notes, the email technologies used and in question at the White House, I'm uniquely suited to conduct this investigation.

It's unlikely any other publisher possesses either the depth of knowledge on both of these technologies or has nearly the level of access we do to the leading technical experts for both systems.

I've personally written more than 600 articles about email, collaboration, and mobile technology. With that many articles, it's likely I've published more articles on email than just about anyone else, anywhere in the world.

Given that I've written extensively about both Microsoft and Lotus email technology for their respective ZATZ publications, I've undoubtedly published more articles about both technologies — combined — than anyone else.

This expertise came in handy for this investigation, where, in addition to all the other issues, I looked at the curious timing behind the White House's migration from Notes to Outlook.

By the time I'd worked my way through the investigation, I wound up involving expertise from four of our five publications.

- The White House initially ran on Lotus Notes, then moved to Outlook, strangely right in the middle of a build-up to war. As the author of *Lotus Notes 3 Revealed!,* the first business book ever on Lotus Notes and as the editor of *DominoPower,* the leading magazine about Lotus Notes and Domino, this story was a perfect fit for editorial coverage.

- The White House currently runs on Microsoft Outlook. As the publisher of *OutlookPower Magazine,* one of the leading publications on email and Microsoft Outlook, I had a unique perspective here as well.

- I'd eventually discover all sorts of interesting problems with the security of Mr. Rove's BlackBerry handheld. As the publishers of *Computing Unplugged Magazine* and before that *PalmPower Magazine,* we here at ZATZ have probably published more articles about handheld personal digital assistants and smartphones than just about any other publisher.

- Even our *Connected Photographer Magazine* got into the act when I found a strange, forged image of Karl Rove floating around the Internet. You'll read about that story later on in the book. It's wacky. I love wacky.

Because I've written so much about all the various products and brands, and because it's professionally necessary for me to remain objective, you can be assured that when I write about one technology or another, you're getting an objective, unbiased, experienced perspective.

I've also done my best to be politically objective. As I told you earlier, I've been on both sides of the partisan fence, and right now, both parties annoy me pretty much equally.

More to the point, our magazine readers expect us to publish technically relevant information. Veering into partisanship is a quick way to lose our audience — and here at ZATZ, we do our best to avoid running the magazines like stupid drunken sailors on crack.

My goal in our editorial coverage of this topic was to make clear the technical elements of the discussion. At ZATZ, we're strictly publishers of technical information, so I've done my best to completely avoid the partisan discussion.

That's not to say I won't involve politics. I'm writing about the White House, after all. And it's also not to say I won't pick on those inside the Beltway. I'll be as equally brutal to Democratic Senators as I am to those currently in the Republican White House.

But I'll only criticize where criticism is warranted. I'll also confine my criticism — pretty much (I'm a politics junky, after all) — to criticism about the technical implementation of the White House's internal messaging infrastructure.

That's more than enough to keep us busy. Some of this crap, I tell you, will curl your hair.

The resources on *EmailsGone.com*

Throughout this book, I've provided Web links to the original documentation and source material used in the investigation.

All of the links in this book are available from the book's Web site. Just visit *EmailsGone.com* and click on the Resources link. That way, you won't have to type in any long URLs.

Web links are notoriously subject to something called "link rot." We've all experienced it. Click a link and instead of going to the page you want, you get an error message.

The government is often guilty of this, especially when administrations change. Information that's available on *WhiteHouse.gov* now will likely be unreachable once the next President takes office.

To make sure all of our source material remains available, I've made PDF (Portable Document Format) electronic copies of all the relevant Web pages and linked to them from *EmailsGone.com*. I've also captured extensive "screen shots" of search results and our forensics process and those extended screen images are also available on *EmailsGone.com*.

Producing this book

This book is unusual for ZATZ because it's coming out in print form. Normally, everything we do is online — including books. Over the years we've published more than fifteen e-books, book-length documents provided in digital form.

Although I got my entrepreneurial start back in 1987 publishing a printed book, this is the first book ZATZ has published in print — and it's the first printed book we've published that derived a lot of its information from material that first appeared online.

Creating this presented some interesting challenges. The first, of course, is that images that can be huge online have to fit onto a printed page. You can't scroll or click a page in a book. In that sense, print is a pretty primitive medium.

I solved that, as described above, by providing the full, original images and source materials on the companion *EmailsGone.com* Web site.

Another interesting challenge was that of publishing style. Technical books look and feel a lot different than books about politics.

Here's one example. Nearly every technical book you're going to find will skip a line between paragraphs and, because there's a skipped line, won't indent the first line of a paragraph. On the other hand, nearly all political books do it old-school. There's no line between paragraphs and each paragraph is indented.

We chose to mix our styles. Our cover is clearly more political than tech. That's important. The magazines reach technical experts. In fact, between our *OutlookPower* and *DominoPower* magazines, we probably reach more active Notes/Domino and Outlook/Exchange experts than any other organization. It's likely that some of them are the people or work for the companies that the government will turn to in order to resolve this technical controversy.

The book has a political cover style because we wanted to reach an audience beyond the million or so techies we reach each week. We wanted to be accessible to politicians and policy makers inside the Beltway and voters throughout the country.

You may have noticed that I've written this book in an informal tone so it'll be fun to read. For example, it should be considered a flagrant grammatical error to use the word "emails" rather than "email" or "email messages." After all, you don't go and pick up your "mails" at the Post Office. You pick up your mail — if you even bother to use snail mail anymore.

However, common usage tends to morph and pervert language. One of the editors here visibly twitches every time she sees the word "emails," but she can't fight it. A Google search on "emails and grammar" finds even the grammar advice sites use the word "emails" now. Which leads me to ask, "Where have all the good Englishes gone?"

If you're really interested in how we (the editors here at ZATZ) produced this book front-to-back, visit *EmailsGone.com* a month or so after the book comes out. We'll have an article series in the magazines that showcases every step of this book's production, from the Photoshop work on the cover to the use of InDesign for page layout, and even how we generated the index.

Acknowledgements

No introduction would be complete without acknowledgements, and I've got a lot to be thankful for.

By far, the biggest thanks has to go to the wonderful, brilliant, lovely, charming, adorable, sweet, simply amazing Denise Amrich. Denise is the managing editor of the ZATZ magazines, our co-founder, and my wife. She has been incredibly supportive of the effort involved with this book, both in a professional capacity, helping to edit and produce the book, as well as in a wiferly capacity, cheering me on, helping to access the risks, and keeping me as sane as I ever get.

Thanks also go to our editors, our more than 300 authors, and our million-plus readers. Many of these people are towering experts in their fields, and they act as a constant peer review body for all our work.

I got some insightful feedback from quite a few of our readers and also help from experts in the messaging industry. Sincere thanks need to go to Roger Matus, Marie Patterson, and Gary Morse for the extensive expertise they provided. You'll learn more directly from them later in the book.

Special thanks also go to the teams at Microsoft and IBM. As expected, when asked about the actual White House installation, both companies clammed up tighter than Fort Knox. But on anything else about Microsoft and IBM products, the product teams at both companies have been infinitely helpful.

Thanks also goes to the National Security Archive of George Washington University. Without their comprehensive records, I wouldn't have been able to find out nearly as much as I did about the early history of email in the White House.

And, finally, a special thanks goes to the folks at both Adobe Systems and Virginia Systems for their helpful support on this project. Adobe kindly supported this project with their InDesign page production technology and, of course, Photoshop, and Virginia Systems provided us with an astounding automatic indexing tool that shaved weeks off our production process.

* * *

Enough with the preliminaries. Prepare to be freaked out...

CHAPTER 1

Prepare to be freaked out

Email at the White House isn't just email, as we normally think of it. Email at the White House is communication at the highest levels of the Executive Branch — deep, candid, often shockingly personal communication within the leadership of the most powerful nation in the world.

When I originally started researching the article series that would become the basis for this book, my plan was to explore what appeared to be some simple questions about email usage and management in the White House.

Instead, I discovered that something as seemingly benign as White House email can have freaky national security consequences.

The tiny little hairs on the back of my neck started to stand up.

Unfortunately, the freaky nature of the problem can be hidden in all the technical arcana of the topic. This seems to be a truth about Washington in general. You have to dig through mounds and mounds of obfuscation to get at the truth — and even when you do, the different tendrils of different truths can wrap around each other, making the whole nearly impossible to untangle.

As I dug deeper into how the White House manages email, knowing what I do about how email works, the tiny little hairs on the back of my neck started to stand up. As I started to think about the implications from the perspective of our nation's security, I realized this was no longer simply about some missing email messages.

Unchecked, some really, *really* bad things could happen.

Since misery loves company, it seems only fair that your stomach should tighten, your mouth go dry, and the hairs on the back of your neck stand at attention as well.

What follows are three possible scenarios. They could be right out of a Tom Clancy novel. The difference between a Clancy novel and what you're about to read is this: these scenarios are based on the real-world problems I discovered in my investigation. What you're about to read could actually happen.

Prepare to be freaked out...

Scenario 1: the attack that backfired

A United States Army Special Forces team is set to attack the secret hideout of a top *al-Qa'idah* operative. The operation has been planned for weeks. No one outside the Special Forces team, Pentagon brass, and senior White House staff knows about the impending attack.

Secrecy is imperative. If even a hint of an attack made its way back to *al-Qa'idah*, our target would vanish into the wind and years of very dangerous human intelligence work would be for naught.

It's 4am in Washington and the attack is about to take place. The President, Chief of Staff, Deputy Chief of Staff, Chairman of the Joint Chiefs, and a variety of deputies are waiting in the super-secure, 5,000 square foot

Situation Room deep within the basement of the West Wing. You can feel the tension in the air.

6,929 miles away, outside the *al-Qa'idah* safe house, the tension is even more palpable. Highly trained American warriors are about to do what they do best. With the President's approval relayed to them, the attack is launched.

And that's when everything starts to go very, very bad.

When the smoke finally clears, all but two of the American soldiers are dead, victims of a diabolical trap. The enemy knew we were coming.

But how? How could they know?

Here's how...

Unknown to all but the White House Deputy Chief of Staff, his assistant, and the IT guy who had to fix the problem, the Deputy Chief of Staff's BlackBerry smartphone had gone missing two days earlier. No one was really concerned about security since this particular White House staffer did mostly political work. That's why he never reported the missing BlackBerry to anyone else.

From the IT guy's perspective, it'd be a pain to hook the DCOS up with a new BlackBerry, but other than that, no great loss.

Except, of course, for the American lives. You see, before it went missing, an email message had been sent to the BlackBerry. The email message contained an attachment. That attachment was a converted Microsoft Word file containing a draft of the press release that would be issued after the attack, for the Deputy Chief of Staff's approval or editing.

Although the press release didn't detail everything about what, by the time it was released to reporters, would have been the over-and-done attack, anyone connected to *al-Qa'idah*, reading it before the attack began, would have been able to piece together some important details — enough to set a trap.

Two days earlier, much of the White House staff had been traveling with the President, staying at a hotel in Tucson, where the President was going to give a well-publicized speech about the environment. Having had only about three hours of sleep (usual for the job), and rushing to catch the plane (also usual for the job), the Deputy Chief of Staff accidentally left his BlackBerry in his hotel room.

When the BlackBerry went missing — retrieved out of the hotel room by a maid with a nephew who had a brother-in-law in *al-Qa'idah*, no one knew that the press release would fall into enemy hands.

After all, it was just a BlackBerry.

Scenario 2: a damaging foreign relations screwup

When dealing with crackpot dictators, subtlety requires you to walk thunderously and use a really big stick. But when dealing with nations like the French Republic, with a history going back to the *Treaty of Verdon* in 843, subtlety is often the best form of diplomacy.

Imagine, for the purposes of our scenario, that the United States is readying for a retaliatory war. Following the dictates of good international relations, the U.S. has sent envoys to its allies, seeking support for an attack. A lot is going on this year, the build-up to war is far from the only thing keeping the White House busy.

The U.S. is already running an invasion in another country, a former FBI agent was caught selling secrets to Moscow, a former U.S. President is flying all over the world, talking to leaders officially on our shit list. We've also got domestic problems, with snipers running around scaring the crap out of our citizens, one of the biggest companies in the world self-destructed, and, oh, there are elections this year as well.

With everything going on internationally and domestically, France's support would be a big help. With their support, we'd seem more on the side of the angels and the invasion we were planning would seem more like a righteous war. France is a very well-respected country and its decisions are known to be tempered with years of maturity. If France throws its support behind an action, you can generally rest assured that the action is well justified.

Of course, it's to our strategic benefit to have world opinion on our side.

France's newly elected leader meets with our ambassador, requesting a five minute courtesy call from the American President. It's a reasonable request considering our countries' mutual good will. Our ambassador passes the request on to the Secretary of State, who has an assistant email the appropriate White House staffer to set up a time for the call.

A week passes with no reply. Given about a thousand other things on his plate, the United States Ambassador to France moves on to other projects and forgets about the request for the call. So does SecState's assistant, who is also just a bit busy.

The French, of course, are sticklers for protocol. They certainly haven't forgotten about the request, but they're also not about to go begging to the U.S. Ambassador for a call from the U.S. President.

Another week passes and a seething *Président de la République Française* is feeling snubbed. This has never happened before. America always replies promptly to such requests. The U.S. has an excellent protocol office and to not get a reply to such a simple courtesy call must be the American President's way of sending some sort of disapproving message to the new French leader.

In the mind of the French president, France doesn't deserve such a snub. Hasn't France been America's longest-running ally? After all, the United States wouldn't have won the Revolutionary War without France's help.

Following a late-night meeting with his *gouvernement* (cabinet of ministers), the French president publicly announces that France cannot support America's planned attack.

It's a huge blow to American foreign relations and to America's reputation worldwide.

But why didn't the White House staffer arrange for the President's call? That's what she does. She arranges things. And she's very good at her job.

It turns out that right in the middle of the build-up to war, some gray-haired Special Assistant to the President decided he didn't like the current email system. It was an email system put in by the previous administration and, as a matter of faith, everything done by the previous administration was bad. So, knowing almost nothing about email systems or IT (Information Technology), the gray-haired old politico ordered the old system yanked and a new system put in its place.

He figured changing things out couldn't be too big a problem. He never used email, but his assistant didn't seem to complain. The kindly old politician knew a senator who knew a techie, the 22-year-old son of one of his contributors, and the 22-year-old geek confirmed that he liked Microsoft more than Lotus anyway.

And so it came to pass that the administration yanked out Lotus Notes from thousands of computers and had to install Outlook. The servers had to change. Everything had to be redone. The staff had to be retrained.

Email, of course, is the lifeblood of internal communications at the White House and, in the middle of this very busy year, a disrupted email system wasn't necessarily helpful. But like all the other challenges of working in these most important of jobs, the staff at the White House took it all in stride.

Unfortunately, a few email messages fell through the cracks. Who cares? If the message is about something important enough, it'll be sent again, right?

Right?

Scenario 3: the ultimate nightmare scenario

Seven months go by. This morning, the President's going to give a fund-raising speech in Palo Alto and then fly from San Francisco International Airport back to Washington. Unknown, however, to everyone but a select few, the President's not going to be driven from Palo Alto directly back to SFO. He's going to detour to the small town of Sunol in the East Bay, population 1,332.

There, the President's going to have a most private conversation with a Senator in the opposing political party. Ever since the last election, when the opposing party won majorities in both the House and Senate, the President's agenda has been hog-tied. But, due to a minor disagreement with a leader in his own party, this particular Senator is thinking of switching sides. If he does, the entire teeter-tottering balance of power in Washington would shift in the President's favor.

All it would take for the Senator to switch is a few promises of political influence — and a face-to-face meeting between the President and the Senator. But no one can know about the meeting until the Senator makes his final decision and announces he's jumped to the President's ship. If word got out before everything was set, the Senator would deny the whole thing and the President's political coup would never happen.

And that's why the President will be taking a very secret detour to Sunol this very morning. Sunol is an out of the way town, and no one will notice one black limo traveling through Niles Canyon for a half-hour conversation over coffee.

Leaving Palo Alto, the bulk of the President's motorcade continues up 101 to the airport. Two unmarked cars, populated with agents of the Presidential Protective Detail, the President in his armored limo, and a helicopter out of Moffet Field bearing commercial markings all turn east, travel over the Dumbarton Bridge, turn right on Mission Boulevard, and head into the narrow Niles Canyon.

Just before the President's limo rounds the curve leading to the Niles Canyon Quarry and the railroad museum, four *Ruchnoy Protivotankovyy Granatomyot* (rocket propelled grenades) smash into the President's structurally-reinforced car. Another two smash into the escort car leading the small caravan and two more destroy the following car. Smoke obscures the area. The overflying helicopter can't see a thing.

The meeting never happens.

But how could anyone have known that the President's limousine would be in the ambush-friendly zone that is Niles Canyon? Security was at its tightest.

There were maybe ten people in the U.S. who knew the meeting was scheduled and the Senator hadn't told anyone, not even his wife or his closest aides.

So how could this have happened?

The leak, it turns out, was a simple email message.

A senior White House official needed to send an email message about the President's visit to another senior White House official. Because the subject was about the political conversion of the Senator, the official knew he wasn't allowed to use the secure government email system. Instead, he was required to use the email system set up for political communication.

No harm in that, right?

No harm, except the system set up for political communication didn't go through secured channels. It was run by a 12-person company in Chattanooga Tennessee. The company knew its stuff, and did a great job of managing email. There was just one gotcha. All such political email had to travel through the public Internet to get to and from the company's servers.

And, as has been the case for the last few years, there was computer in the back of a store on Broad Street, just a few doors down from the Chattanooga company managing the President's political email. Connected to the computer was a simple DSL connection to BellSouth. Nothing fancy — except that the upstream network provider to the political ISP (Internet service provider) was also BellSouth.

The computer in the back of the store on Broad Street simply "sniffed" all the network packets it could find, hoping for a whiff of something yummy. This was possible since nearly everything that travels over the Internet is easy to intercept. The wide-open nature of Internet protocols made the Internet easy to design initially, but has long been a fatal flaw from the perspective of security.

Some of the packets the computer sniffed could be reconstructed into email messages. And one of the email messages the computer reconstructed just happened to be one from the one White House staffer to the other White House staffer. Since the Internet is generally open and unsecured, especially when it comes to email, it was really easy to intercept these particular email messages.

Of course, the computer in the back of that store on Broad Street wasn't being operated by anyone with affection for the U.S. government. It was one of the many off-the-shelf PCs bought and placed throughout the country, constantly scanning, hoping to capture something juicy. Something that could be used to hurt America.

This particular message detailed the White House staffer's excitement about the upcoming Niles Canyon road trip. After all, Charlie Chaplin filmed *The Champ* in Niles Canyon and this staffer loved the historical significance.

Littled did our staffer know that, just a few days later, Niles Canyon would forever be known for something far more horrible.

Truth and fiction

The three scenarios you've just read are, thankfully, pure fiction.

Unfortunately, these scenarios are far more possible than anyone knew. They are based on the disturbing, yet verifiable details about White House email operations I discovered over the course of my investigation.

For example, reading deep into transcripts of Congressional testimony, I learned that Karl Rove, who at the time was Deputy Chief of Staff to President George W. Bush, lost his BlackBerry handheld phone more than once.

I was shocked to discover that, during the 2002-2003 build-up to the Iraq war, the Executive Office of the President decided to replace its Lotus Notes email infrastructure with Microsoft Outlook. This migration clearly interrupted email flow in the White House, leading to an April 13, 2007 statement where White House Deputy Press Secretary Dana Perino implied than possibly five million email messages got lost in the transition.

Over the course of my investigation, I've learned that White House staffers are often not legally allowed to take advantage of all the security the United States government can offer. Instead, because of the antiquated Hatch Act of 1939, I estimate that more than 103.6 million White House email messages have been sent over the open Internet, via SMARTech, a 12-person Internet service provider located in downtown Chattanooga.

This investigation began over a political issue: a Democratically-held Congress demanded email from the White House, looking for evidence that former Attorney General Alberto Gonzales was party to the dismissal of eight U.S. Attorneys in 2006.

While I did find very real concerns about White House email archiving and missing email messages, I found other flaws in the system that could, hopefully never — but still possibly — lead to the nightmares described above.

A history of controversy

Unfortunately, my discoveries weren't limited by just national security problems. I found a history of controversy — and some very strange people connections.

I found controversy over how the White House uses email dating back 25 years, almost as far back as email's very existence. Despite the intent of both the Presidential Records Act and the Federal Records Act, all White House administrations from Reagan on have tried to hide or destroy their email.

In Reagan's time, National Security Advisor John Poindexter did a late night run, attempting to delete email incriminating both himself and Ollie North in criminal activities. He was later convicted, and even later wound up in charge of George W. Bush's "total information awareness" program.

Also, in Reagan's time, a Deputy Attorney General named John Bolton argued for the administration's right to destroy all the email from the Reagan presidency. Although overruled in court, Bolton (whose long-time criticism of the United Nations "Goes a long way past healthy scepticism," according to the BBC) would eventually wind up as Ambassador to the U.N., appointed by George W. Bush while Congress was in recess.

At the very end of George H. W. Bush's presidency, a deal was struck between the then President and Don W. Wilson, the Archivist of the United States, to allow for 4,852 Bush I administration backup tapes to be bundled into boxes and then into vans in the middle of the night, hours before Bill Clinton's inauguration. The tapes eventually wound up at the Bush Presidential Library in Texas, Wilson was discredited in court and lost his job as Archivist. A few weeks later, he wound up as Executive Director of the Bush Presidential Library.

While we're on the topic of weird people connections, another one came to our attention while I was investigating SMARTech, the 12-person ISP in Tennessee that runs much of the Republican National Committee's Internet services. The connection gets weird because Ohio's then Secretary of State (the person who oversee's Ohio's elections) was a Republican named Ken Blackwell. Mr. Blackwell was running for Governor of Ohio.

Mr. Blackwell became nationally known in 2004. He had two clearly conflicting roles. He was the chief elections official of Ohio and honorary co-chair of the Committee to Re-elect George W. Bush during the 2004 election. Mr. Blackwell also served under the first President Bush as Undersecretary of Department of Housing and Urban Development.

While looking into SMARTech, I saw that the Office of Federal Housing Enterprise Oversight, part of Housing and Urban Development, hosted its Web site on their servers. I also found Ohio election files on SMARTech's servers.

I find it curious that official state election documents appear on a SMARTech server. It's also curious that the senior election official in Ohio was also running for Governor of Ohio while this went on. It's further somewhat curious that a finance oversight agency of HUD runs its Web site on SMARTech's servers and that Mr. Blackwell was previously undersecretary of HUD.

But the weird isn't limited to the Bush administrations. President Bill Clinton's staff tried to change the National Security Council from being considered an agency, thereby preventing Freedom of Information Act requests on NSC communications.

Everything eventually came full circle — back to Alberto Gonzales. Executive Order 13,233, drafted by then White House Council Alberto Gonzales under President George W. Bush, gives any sitting president new privileges with regard to records. It allows a president to restrict access to these documents — virtually forever.

Deep flaws

Unfortunately, my discoveries weren't limited by just national security problems or weird people connections. I found deep, intrinsic flaws in how email is managed.

Email is often more personal than a formal letter, and since email messages are mostly in written form, email is more tangible than a phone call. As such, the accumulated email messages of a White House administration are ideal for digital archeologists, digging for insight (and dirt) on an administration.

It's a tough call: the law requires all Presidential email to be archived. And yet, exposed to public view, an administration's email records could prove to be a potent weapon for the opposition. Sift through anyone's email and you're going to find at least one inappropriate or idiotic message. Given the hundreds of millions of email messages that make up the official email record of an administration, you're bound to find one or two that are incredibly embarrassing.

Is it any wonder that White House administrations aren't looking for the best tools for archiving messages? If you're not sure you want email messages to come to light in a prewar build-up, migrate to a new email system. So, five million or so messages get lost. Big deal. Blame it on the migration to a new email system.

If you don't want all your political messages to be archived, just allow those in the Executive Office of the President to press Delete. Oops. Message gone.

And, if the fuss finally becomes too much, agree to revamp your email archiving methodology. Rather than using an archiving server, a technology expressly designed to solve this problem, you might choose to use the approach described by Deputy White House Press Secretary Dana Perino.

In April 2007, she suggested:

> *So you would either print it off, or you would forward it to another email, to your personal account — I'm sorry, to your White House account, in some way keep that so that in the future, if the Counsel's Office needed to look back at those records, that they would have access to that.*

Clearly, the White House isn't taking their email problems seriously at all. That plan isn't even remotely realistic. Can you imagine yourself doing that?

Our next steps

As email professionals, my colleagues and I have been shocked by what I've uncovered. As American citizens, we're deeply concerned by the implications.

Over the course of this book, you'll learn everything I learned. I'll take you through all the steps of my investigation, the digital forensics, the smoking-gun evidence, the political gambits played by our last four Presidents to keep you from learning the truth, the mind-blowingly bad management, and the very real (and very dangerous) national security disasters-in-waiting I've discovered.

Are you freaked out yet?

Fortunately, the scenarios described can be avoided completely. Before you're done with this book, you'll understand the three root causes of the White House email problem and you'll also understand how my six very doable recommendations can quickly and easily bring security and safety back to White House email.

Read on. It's a heck of a story.

Tips from the ZATZ magazines

The BlackBerry isn't the only smartphone, according to *Computing Unplugged Magazine*.

If you're looking for a smartphone, you might also want to consider a Treo from Palm or a Microsoft Windows Mobile device.

Don't forget though: if you get a smartphone, you'll gain quality Internet access and the ability to control what software is on your phone, but there will be extra fees for Internet data access. You may need to check with your IT people first.

CHAPTER 2

A historical perspective

Recent media coverage makes it seem like the fuss over White House email is unique to the George W. Bush White House. Nothing could be further from the truth. I gave you a preview of that in Chapter 1. But there's a whole lot more to the story. Controversy over how the White House uses email dates back almost as far as email's very existence.

Controversy over how the White House uses email dates back almost as far as email's very existence.

Way before the Internet, way before Outlook or Lotus Notes, way before Web browsers, Hotmail, Gmail, or even cc:Mail, there was email in use at the White House. And there was controversy. According to the National Security Archive of George Washington University:

President Ronald Reagan tried to erase the White House email computer backup tapes during his last week in office, in January 1989.

President George Bush [the first] signed a secret deal with the Archivist of the United States just before midnight on his last day in office, in January 1993 — an attempt to put the White House email under seal and take it with him to Texas.

*President Bill Clinton reversed forty years of legal precedent in March
1994 by defining the National Security Council out of existence as an
"agency" of the U.S. Government, in an attempt to put the White House
email beyond the reach of the Freedom of Information Act.*

As best as we can tell, it all starts with Ollie North, Ronald Reagan, and a
former scientist named Poindexter...

Flashback: Reagan administration (1981-1989)

Among the nearly one million readers of the ZATZ magazines, some are
old-school techies. While the youngest of our readers don't remember a world
without cell phones, some of the old-timers remember early email systems.
And one of IBM's earliest email systems was PROFs (the Professional Office
System).

Time has a way of blurring our memories. In today's political climate,
President Reagan is often pointed to as the model President of the modern
conservative movement. And while Ronald Reagan was in this author's
opinion a great President, his administration was also flawed — and racked
with controversy.

In fact, it was controversy over something called Iran-Contra that starts all
the fuss. This isn't the place for a formal history lesson, but the basics are this.
In the mid-1980s, members of the Reagan administration sold arms to Iran.
The money from these sales was funneled to *contrarevolucionarios* in South
America known as the Contras.

Without a doubt, it was one of the dumber foreign policy plans the U.S. has
come up with in recent years — and America has not suffered a shortage of
dumb foreign policy plans. As some of you might remember, the whole wildly
convoluted Iran-Contra Affair landed like a ton of bricks, sending Reaganauts

scrambling and firing up a whole round of 80s-style congressional hearings. Your tax dollars at work, 1980s edition.

It turns out that back in 1982, the NSC (National Security Council) acquired an early version of PROFs. That relatively primitive email system was originally released by IBM just a year earlier. In those days, email at the White House was really a prototype, sort of a *beta*, in today's terms.

It wasn't until April of 1985 that email became a fully-integrated system among the various departments and was in wide use by White House staffers. It's there that our story really begins to get some traction.

Email was new enough and ephemeral enough to seem like a safe back channel for communication.

Before we really begin to dig into the details, let's stop for a moment and clarify some references. This book, and especially this chapter, is going to be talking about Presidents Reagan, Bush, Clinton, and Bush — and those dual mentions of Bush father and son are likely to get confusing.

For the purpose of editorial clarity, and with all due respect to the Bush Presidents, when I mention Bush I or the Bush I administration, I'm speaking of George Herbert Walker Bush, the 41st President of the United States, the father. When I mention Bush II or the Bush II administration, I'm speaking of George W. Bush, the 43rd President of the United States, the son of Bush I.

Now that we've got our Presidents straight, let's continue this fascinating story.

Iran-Contra began to melt down in November 1986. While printed documents and memos traveled through official government channels and were clearly subject to Presidential Records Act oversight, email was new enough and ephemeral enough to seem like a safe back channel for communication.

Back then, the National Security Advisor was Rear Admiral John Poindexter, a CalTech Ph.D. Weirdly enough, Poindexter would go on to write a multi-tasking symbolic debugger (program code used to fix problems in computer programs), a BBS (bulletin board system, sort of a precursor to today's online discussion forums), and a pile of PC utility programs in the mid-1990s. Writing little PC applications is not exactly how you'd expect to find a former National Security Advisor spending his time, but that's what he did.

In any case, back in November 1986, Poindexter was working hard with Lieutenant Colonel Oliver North to shred all sorts of incriminating Iran-Contra documentation. During this time, while Poindexter and North were doing their best to get rid of their paper trail, they were using email, a process they called "Private Blank Check," to keep in touch. Former National Security Advisor Robert "Bud" McFarlane also participated in this process even after leaving the White House. He emailed White House staffers from a terminal (remember those?) in his house.

Once Poindexter and North were done shredding paper documents, they got to "shredding" digital documents. North deleted 750 out of 758 email messages and Poindexter deleted 5,012 out of 5,062 messages. Poindexter also knew about backups. Backup tapes in the White House were recycled every two weeks, so he knew that if he just kept deleting messages for a while, even the backup tapes would be overwrittten.

What Poindexter didn't realize was that a number of White House career civil service employees were onto his game. One such civil servant, Patrick M. McGovern, also a Lieutenant Colonel like North, told his staff to set aside copies of the backup tapes. FBI agents soon commissioned data dumps for the backup tapes, the email messages were made public during the Tower Commission hearings, and some very juicy White House email was being read by Americans in the mid-1980s.

On April 7, 1990, John Marlan Poindexter was convicted on multiple felony counts on for conspiracy, obstruction of justice, perjury, defrauding the government, and the alteration and destruction of evidence pertaining to the Iran-Contra Affair.

Poindexter never did serve any jail time because the convictions were later overturned on a technicality.

Strangely enough, in 2003 Poindexter wound up back in government service for the Bush II administration as Director of the DARPA IAO (Defense Advanced Projects Agency Information Awareness Office), an agency funded to develop "total information awareness" technologies that could lead to mass-surveillance systems.

So the guy who was convicted on multiple felony counts for conspiracy, obstruction of justice, perjury, defrauding the government, and the alteration and destruction of evidence pertaining to the Iran-Contra Affair was now in charge of "total information awareness."

Yep, the guy who did his best to avoid being watched in his actions with Iran-Contra was now developing the mother of all surveillance systems for the Bush II administration. That's a head scratcher.

Keeping Reagan's email records

By the end of the Reagan administration in 1989, most of the Executive Office of the President was online with email and more than seven million email messages resided in White House systems. But the fun doesn't stop with the end of the Reagan administration. In fact, it's the end of the Reagan administration that opens up the next stage of White House email fun.

It's always the geeks who get in the way.

See, back then, the White House didn't consider email to be "records" and so, as the Reagan staffers were leaving their offices for the last time, they were getting ready to completely destroy all of the email from the eight years of the Reagan White House.

It's always the geeks who get in the way.

A guy named Eddie Becker worked for the National Security Archive of George Washington University. He'd been following the Iran-Contra Affair for his bosses and was curious about what was going to happen to the Reagan-era email records. After doing a little digging, he was shocked to find out that the National Archives & Records Administration (NARA) didn't consider email "records".

NARA was going to do nary a thing and, except for those email messages set aside for legal cases, all the rest were scheduled for "disposal" the night before Bush I was to be inaugurated.

Now, here's where it gets particularly juicy. Eddie's bosses decided to make a Freedom of Information Act request for all of the Reagan-era email and sued the government to prevent destruction. Amazingly, this all happened almost immediately. At 5:15pm on January 19, 1989 in U.S. District Court, in front of the honorable (late) Barrington D. Parker, Civil Action No. 89-142 was about to be adjudicated.

What makes it juicy? The guy representing the U.S. Government, defending its right to destroy all these emails, was none other than the mustachioed John Bolton, who, 16 years later in 2005, was perhaps the warmest personality to ever be nominated for U.S. Ambassador to the United Nations.

The Senate wouldn't confirm Bolton as Ambassador, in part due to his claim in 1994 that "There is no such thing as the United Nations." He also stated, according to *The Washington Post*, "The Secretariat building in New York has 38 stories. If you lost ten stories today, it wouldn't make a bit of difference."

Even so, while Congress was in recess and couldn't legally argue the matter, on August 1, 2005, Bush II appointed John Robert Bolton as U.S. Ambassador to the United Nations and Permanent Representative. He lasted as Permanent Representative for a little over a year.

Back in 1989, this same John R. Bolton was an assistant Attorney General. It was Bolton who sat at the defense table, trying to make sure the government had a right to destroy all of the Reagan-era email messages.

At 6:10pm, on the eve of Bush I's inauguration, Judge Barrington D. Parker issued a Temporary Restraining Order, prohibiting the destruction of the backup tapes to the Reagan-era PROFs system. The National Security Archives managed to keep those email messages from being destroyed, but it began a court battle that lasted through all four years of the Bush I administration.

Flashback: Bush I administration (1989-1993)

Most of us remember the four years of the first Bush administration. It was a busy time. Operation Just Cause deposed Manuel Noriega as dictator of Panama. With 25,000 troops, the Panama invasion was the largest American troop movement since Vietnam.

After Saddam Hussein invaded Kuwait, Operations Desert Shield and Desert Storm bookmarked the first Iraqi war, knocking Saddam out of Kuwait, but stopping short of deposing the Iraqi leader — in retrospect, probably a smart move.

The Soviet Union was falling apart, and President Bush and Mikhail Gorbachev declared a strategic partnership at a summit in 1991. Much of NAFTA (the North American Free Trade Agreement) was negotiated during Bush I's tenure.

Perhaps most controversial of all were two key themes: the U.S. economy was hurting and Bush I pardoned six Reagan officials implicated in Iran-Contra.

As it pertains to email, not much new happened in the first Bush administration — at least until the very end. For the full four years, the case between the government and National Security Archive was processed through the U.S. District Court and the U.S Court of Appeals.

At the end of 1992, when Bush I lost his re-election bid to Bill Clinton, U.S. District Court Judge Charles R. Richey granted a motion to include the Bush I White House email backups in the case. In January 1993, Richey ruled that email had to be treated like other government records. This treatment includes coverage by law, management by archivists, and preservation.

Apparently, things started to get interesting when the outgoing Bush I people were facing the prospect of an incoming Clinton team. On the eve of President Clinton's inauguration, once again on a January 19th evening, this time in 1993, staffers in the outgoing Bush I administration got their busy on.

According to the National Security Archive, a group of National Archives & Records Administration employees rented vans, drove them to the Old Executive Office Building, assembled hand-written inventories, and loaded 4,852 computer tapes into boxes and then into the vans, with the backup tapes destined for the Bush Presidential Library in Texas.

While this was going on, Bush I was doing a deal with the Archivist of the United States, Don (not "The Dragon") Wilson. Just hours before Bill Clinton was to be sworn in, the agreement gave Bush I control over all the backup tapes, completely bypassing The Presidential Records Act.

So, where did the discredited former Archivist of the United States wind up?

Wilson was already in trouble with Judge Richey for "abdicating his duties as Archivist" because he allowed the destruction the Reagan-era email records. From Judge Richey's perspective, this last minute Bush/Wilson deal to bypass the Presidential Records Act was the icing on the cake. Threatened with an in-depth investigation, Wilson resigned.

So, where did the discredited former Archivist of the United States wind up after attempting to destroy both the Reagan presidential email records and the Bush presidential email records? Three weeks after the midnight ride of the email vans, Don W. Wilson accepted a gig as Executive Director of the Bush Presidential Library Center.

Flashback: Clinton administration (1993-2001)

Just in case you think the White House email controversy is limited to Republicans and this book represents a witch hunt by a liberal-leaning media, let me set you straight. The Democratic Clinton administration committed its own series of no-nos when it came to email.

In fact, when it comes to hiding email from the public, the Clinton administration is the clear spiritual successor to the previous Republican administrations.

You might think Clinton officials would want the Reagan and Bush I email records to see the light of day, but not so much. Instead, in early 1993, Clinton officials appeared at the U.S. Court of Appeals supporting not only the Reagan and Bush I arguments for destroying email records, but also in support of the agreement between Bush I and Archivist Wilson.

Even their reasoning was the same: political paranoia. Clinton administration Senior Advisor on Policy and Strategy George Stephanopoulos is quoted in the May 18, 1993 issue of *The Washington Post* as saying "Like Bush's White House, the Clinton White House does not want a succceeding, potentially unfriendly administration pawing through its computer memos."

In August 1993, the U.S. Court of Appeals ruled against the Clinton White House, stating that White House email qualified as records and should be treated as such under the law.

You'd think that'd be all. Email messages had again been judged as records and, by order of the Court, all such email records must be preserved. Not so fast, bucko. The Clinton White House had some other ideas. And they were sneaky.

You see, although the law applied to email, the question was whether the Presidential Records Act law applied or the Federal Records Act law applied. The difference is that Federal Records Act law applies to *agencies*. Agencies are subject to the Freedom of Information Act. Presidential records are not.

In order for you or I to be permitted — by a Freedom of Information Act filing — to see the records of the National Security Council, the NSC would have to be considered an agency. For almost 50 years, since 1947, it *was* considered an agency — that is, until March, 1994.

On March 25, 1994, President Clinton filed papers declaring that the National Security Council is *not* an agency, therefore is *not* subject to Freedom of Information Act regulations — keeping all Clinton-era NSC email records out of public view.

In 1995, Judge Richey rejected this approach, claiming the Clinton administration's attempts to reclassify the National Security Council as "arbitrary and capricious...contrary to history, past practice, and the law."

That should have been the end of it. As you might imagine, it was not.

Bush II administration (2001-2009)

We'll be covering a lot of what's going on in the Bush II administration later in this book, but one aspect of Bush II activities directly relates to the historical perspective covered in this chapter. On November 1, 2001, Bush II issued Executive Order 13,233, which effectively overturns the disclosure requirements for the Presidential Records Act.

You need to understand something about the Presidential Records Act. Even though information is intended to be disclosed to American citizens, any former President can restrict access to that information for a period of up to 12 years after leaving office.

It allows the President to restrict access to these documents — virtually forever.

There are some minor loopholes in this, primarily to protect real national security concerns. The law also requires all confidential and private communication between the President and his advisors to be made available, without any exception for "attorney-client" or "attorney work product" documents.

President Reagan's records could (theoretically) be viewed in 2001, Bush I's records could (theoretically) be viewed in 2005, Bill Clinton's records in 2013, and Bush II's records in 2021.

Executive Order 13,233, drafted by Bush II's then White House Council Alberto Gonzales (yes, the very same guy about whom the entire White House email controversy began), gives the President (any President) new privileges with regard to records. It allows the President to restrict access to these documents — virtually forever.

Think about the reason for the PRA. It's meant to allow the public, long after a President has left office, to really see what went on. This new Executive Order prevents citizens from *ever* gaining a clear view of the inner workings of a given presidency.

The new Executive Order also changes how someone can gain access to information. In the past, information was disclosed for any reason. Now, the requestor has to prove a "demonstrated, specific need" for the materials.

Additionally, the law states that management of the records is governed by the Archivist of the United States. With the new Executive Order, it's up to the President to decide where and when information requests should be honored.

Further, the new Executive Order allows an incumbent President to block release of documents from a former President. So, for example, Bush II can (and has) blocked the release of documents from the administration of his father.

The new Executive Order also blocks any attempt by Congress at oversight. The Archivist is forbidden to make presidential records available unless both the incumbent and former President authorize access. In the case of former Presidents who have died, their "designated representative" can act on behalf of the President for the purposes of the Act and the Executive Order.

Finally, while the Presidential Records Act also governs the records of Vice Presidents, the new Executive Order allows a former Vice President to make a claim of executive privilege to bar access to materials, and, at that time, the Archivist is required to withhold access to materials until such time that the former Vice President allows the materials to be made public or a court orders it.

I don't know about you, but I can't imagine that ever happening.

Bits of history, final thoughts

This chapter purposely takes us outside of our investigation into the current White House email practices and brings *all* White House email into a more historical perspective. What we've seen is that all administrations, Republican and Democrat, Conservative and Liberal — all of them — have attempted to restrict access to email messages.

We've all sent hundreds, if not thousands, of email messages. As a group, White House staffers send millions. Among all those messages are bound to be a few that are inappropriate, stupid, illegal, or otherwise embarrassing. It is a natural urge to restrict access to such communication just because none of us could stand up to the scrutiny.

Among all those messages are bound to be a few that are inappropriate, stupid, illegal, or otherwise embarrassing.

But America runs on scrutiny. The whole thing relies on a system of checks and balances. The Founding Fathers knew that people, especially people in power, can be corrupt, dumb, silly, and... well... human. If any one branch of the government is allowed to run unchecked, very bad things can happen. Even with checks and balances, administrations have screwed up.

Whether it was Andrew Jackson's deluded decision to sign the Indian Removal Act into law in 1830 (effectively deporting 45,000 American Indians to the West), Franklin Roosevelt's Executive Order 9066 (which authorized the internment of 120,000 American citizens of Japanese descent), President Kennedy's poorly thought out invasion of Cuba (the Bay of Pigs Fiasco), Richard Nixon's collected crimes of Watergate, Ronald Reagan's Iran-Contra, Bill Clinton and the Blue Dress, or even WMDs in Iraq, Presidents have made mistakes.

They've also inspired us, led us, fought for us, and changed our world — often for the better.

It is essential that we be able to see into the past, to be able to see into the operations of former administrations, and to have access, as a citizenry, to the detailed minutiae of presidential operations. After all, the only way we'll learn not to do our own dumb things is to understand what's come before.

Sometimes, we might even learn how to do things better and smarter. After all, not everyone has a perfect memory. But if we have access to all the presidential records, future generations can learn from Ronald Reagan, Bill Clinton, the two Bushes, and the best and brightest of their staff — and the Presidents and staff of future administrations. Without those records, we might have to learn the tough lessons all over again.

I've done my best here to not be political. When I started writing about the history of White House email, I had no idea that I'd discover a convicted felon had been put in charge of DARPA's Information Awareness Office or that a wildly unpopular (and slightly creepy) U.N. ambassador was the the guy who once fought to destroy all of the Reagan-era email records.

But when you do research, weird stuff shows up. And I'd be remiss if I didn't tell you about it. So there's politics in this story. That's because there's politics in presidential history.

I couldn't make this stuff up.

Acknowledgement

Finally, I want to send a special shoutout to the National Security Archive of George Washington University. Without their comprehensive records and their book, *White House e-mail,* published in 1995, I wouldn't have found a fraction of the information in this chapter.

Online resources

All of the links in this book are available from the book's Web site. Just visit *EmailsGone.com* and click on the Resources link. That way, you won't have to type in any long URLs.

Visit the National Security Archive of George Washington University at *http://www.gwu.edu/~nsarchiv/index.html*.

Read Executive Order 13,233 at *http://www.whitehouse.gov/news/releases/2001/11/20011101-12.html*.

Read more about the book, *White House e-mail,* at *http://www.gwu.edu/~nsarchiv/white_house_email/index.html*.

CHAPTER 3

Can email messages just disappear?

As we've discovered, email at the White House isn't just email as we normally think of it. Email at the White House is communication at the highest levels of the Executive Branch, communication within the leadership of the most powerful nation in the world. A breakdown in communication can be a very *baaaad* thing when you're talking about people who have their fingers on The Button.

If something goes wrong with email at the White House, the whole world could be in a whole world of hurt.

In this chapter, I'm going to look at how many messages may be missing and then deconstruct some of the damning assertions made by the loyal opposition about how email messages can't just disappear. But first, let's talk about the "deer-in-the-headlights" look that technical topics tend to inspire.

I was at a dinner party recently where I briefly discussed my research for this book. The guests were quite technically literate; one even worked for IBM. And yet, as I began to touch on the scope of the White House email problem, I could see eyes beginning to glaze over.

Email has reached the point where it's annoying familiar to most of us. Even so, the true details of how email actually works are poorly understood by most people. Most Americans — Senators included — get the bulk of their forensics knowledge from TV shows like *Law & Order.* Reality is a bit more complex and that's partially why a book like this is necessary — to help people better understand what's really happening. But, if I were to simply jump into the tech of disappearing messages and all the other email intricacies we need to cover without giving you some background, your eyes might also glaze over.

Throughout the book, I've done my best to explain everything so it's easy to read and easy to understand. If one or two concepts seem a little tough to grasp, don't worry. It'll all become clear over time.

I promise to be gentle.

By the time you're done reading this chapter, you'll find out whether Senator Leahy's got a clue about what can happen to email and whether Jon Stewart's rearranging White House statements just to get a laugh.

But it's not all partisan politics and late night comedy. Email is critically important to our infrastructure. Email, in our 21st century world, is a glue that holds us together. Email allows us to communicate asynchronously with other people. In other words, I can write an email message at my convenience, say at 4am, and you can read it at your convenience, say at 1pm the next day.

Business runs on email. So does much of the White House. The difference is this: if we here at ZATZ make an error and a message doesn't go through, or a message gets lost, the damage is containable. In most cases, it's easily recoverable. Even in the worst case, a finite number of people will be affected.

But if something goes wrong with email at the White House, the whole world could be in a whole world of hurt.

By digging into this issue, I've uncovered some troubling questions. I've found that millions of messages from White House personnel are likely traveling "in the open," without any security. I've found that archiving strategies for email in the Executive Office of the President are so bad as to be almost silly.

And I've also seen obfuscation and confusion at all levels. That's part of why this book is here, to help you peel away the layers of technical mumbo-jumbo so you can understand the strategic issues underlying this seemingly mind-numbing topic.

The White House has never explicitly confirmed that messages are missing

This book, of necessity, has to be about politics. After all, I'm discussing White House practices. It is, however, very carefully not partisan. I've come at this issue from a technical perspective and have been very careful to avoid taking any sides.

But that doesn't mean I'm not going to be critical of both sides. As we've seen, both Democrats and Republicans have weaseled in their approach to managing email. In this chapter, it'll seem like I'm mostly picking on the Democrats. In future chapters, I'll be asking tough questions of the Republicans in the White House. A good time will be had by all.

By the way, I'm going to repeat my "this is not a partisan issue" message from time to time. One of the things I've learned from my magazine writing is that as soon as I even begin to veer into topics like politics and religion, some people almost automatically flip out. I've learned, however, that if I just regularly repeat the mantra that I'm not being political, but exploring a topic that touches on politics, my intention sinks in and those same people calm right down and often contribute valuable perspectives.

Since not everyone is going to read this book from beginning to end, I'm going to regularly sprinkle scene-setting messages like "this is not a partisan issue" throughout the book. If you're reading straight through the book, well, a little repetition can also help reinforce that message.

America's safety and security is vitally important to us all, so the topics covered in this book are important. No matter what party you side with, there are strategies here that can make for a more secure White House.

This whole book is about how politics and technology dance together. It's a lack of understanding and a lack of commitment to good technology practice that's caused the problems we're discussing at the White House.

The next few sections in this chapter and the subsequent chapters in the book will help you understand the key elements of email technology. Armed with this knowledge, you'll be much better prepared to prevent such problems in the future.

But now, let's get back to the topic of missing email messages.

How much email are we talking about?

Apparently, the White House manages a "massive number" of email messages any year. In the April 16 White House Press Briefing, Deputy Press Secretary Dana Perino described the numbers as follows:

> *And, remember, there's a huge amount of email that comes in and out of the White House. And it's quite a feat for the IT folks to be able to keep up with software upgrades and storage and the amount of — just the amount of traffic that's coming in and out on emails. On any given year, I think I've read upwards of 50 million emails are sent and received, not*

to mention forwarded or copied or blind copied, or all of those different features that you can use with email. So it's a massive number.

Hah! Those folks at the White House are such lightweights.

Here at ZATZ, we send and receive more than 54 million email messages each year, well over a million a week. We have a *lot* of subscribers.

We manage four million more email messages a year than the White House and we don't have the full resources of the United States government at our disposal.

The claim, however, is that there are close to five million email messages missing. In that same Press Briefing, Ms. Perino stated:

> *I don't have a specific number for you. Again, I wouldn't rule out that there were a potential 5 million emails lost, but we'll see if we can get to you. If it was 5 million, I think that, again, out of 1,700 people using email every day, again, there was no intent to have lost them.*

She also said:

> *We're not talking about GWB emails, but within the EOP system, that there had been a gap or that there had been upwards of 5 million emails that were missing. Scott and I are looking into that; we're talking to the Office of Administration.*

Scott, in this case, is Scott Stanzel, another Deputy Press Secretary at the White House. In future chapters, we'll talk about what she means by "GWB emails" and "EOP emails."

It's important to be clear when reading these statements that, at no time, does the White House explicitly confirm messages are missing. If you read the transcripts carefully, you'll see these statements are in response to assertions by outside political groups. Thus far, however, the White House has neither confirmed nor denied that a large amount of messages subject to the Presidential Records Act are actually missing. In fact, we may never know.

It's very difficult nailing down the truth, or even finding a bread crumb path to the truth, especially since there's so much distortion in the media.

Denise and I greatly enjoy watching the *Daily Show with Jon Stewart*, which we did on April 16, the night when one of these Press Briefings took place.

On the show, Stewart showed a clip of Perino saying "I wouldn't rule out that there were a potential 5 million emails lost" and then a few seconds later, after editorializing on the amount five million, he aired a clip showing her saying:

Well, I will admit it, we screwed up and we're trying to fix it.

Watching the program, you'd think she went from saying she wouldn't rule out the potential of five million messages lost and then admitted they'd screwed up by losing the messages.

But the fact is, although Ms. Perino talked about the five million messages on Monday, April 16th, the statement about screwing up was made the previous Thursday. It actually came from the April 12 White House Press Briefing.

And, she wasn't talking about screwing up by losing five million messages. She'd just finished talking about the policy of archiving RNC political email, which was a related, but different, technical problem.

My analysis throughout this process has shown that email management within the Executive Office of the President is fundamentally flawed, and has been across administrations. There's no doubt this isn't good and needs to be fixed. But the process of understanding is made vastly harder when everyone, Left and Right, Republican and Democrat, mainstream media and blogger, are all distorting the facts for their own agenda.

It's starting to piss me off.

Looking at how hard it was to find the grains of truth from an event that was barely a month old when I first started researching it, it's fascinating to me that historians are able to claim that they can reconstruct historical events from hundreds or even thousands of years ago. An archeologist finds a clay pot in the desert and all of a sudden, we have a complete history of an ancient civilization.

I don't think so.

In fact, I'm beginning to think that every discussion of history should begin with a disclaimer: *Uh, well, see, we have no real idea what happened here, but we're makin' some wild-ass guesses. Based on these guesses, we've come up with a heck of a story. Now, let me tell you about the Battle of Thermopylae...*

Deconstructing a possible loss of email messages

In response to the allegations of missing emails, Senate Judiciary Commitee Chairman Patrick Leahy (D-VT) made the following statement:

> *You can't erase emails, not today. They've gone through too many servers. They can't say they've been lost. That's like saying, "The dog ate my homework."*

Unfortunately, Senator Leahy's statement is flawed. Never underestimate the ability of technology to fail in interesting and spectacular ways. The Senator is really making three technical statements:

- Email messages can't be erased.

- Email messages traversing servers are stored as they go through the server.

- Email messages can't be lost.

"You can't erase emails, not today."

The Outlook email program uses a variety of mechanisms for storing email messages. One of the most common is the use of Personal Folder Storage files, also known as PST files. A PST file is a digital computer file stored on a user's hard drive that contains a collection of email messages. Think of it as a database of email. These messages can be organized, sorted — and deleted.

If an email message is stored in a PST file, the email message, when first deleted, drops into the Deleted Items folder. This is really just another folder for email storage within the PST file. It serves as a holding bin, someplace where it's easy to find a message that was deleted (often accidentally) and return it to regularly use.

To more permanently delete a message, you'd delete the message from the Deleted Items folder. If an email message is deleted from the Deleted Items folder, it's no longer available for you to retrieve, but the message data may still exist in the PST file and if it hasn't been overwritten (a big if), it could be retrieved using a variety of file recovery and analysis tools.

This is the concept of the double-delete, something we'll talk more about in future chapters. The first delete moves the message to the Deleted Items folder and the second delete removes it from the user's reach, waiting for Outlook to eventually reclaim the disk storage space taken by the message.

Ironically, email messages often also get lost when Outlook auto-archives messages. The auto-archive mechanism exists to reduce the space used in the main PST file, and at the same time save a copy of the message. But rather than helping a user keep older messages, the auto-archive feature often has the opposite effect.

We've had many reports from users who lost their archive files when moving to a new machine after letting Outlook auto-archive messages. Generally, it was because they remembered to move their Personal Folders.PST files (the main email message database file), but forgot to move their archive files, which were living somewhere in the Documents and Settings folder.

Another way messages can get lost or erased on a user's personal computer is damage to the file. The PST file itself can be deleted, damaged, or destroyed. This is a common complaint readers send into us at *OutlookPower Magazine*.

In a corporate environment, email messages often reside on a centralized server. This isn't a universal case, however. Many laptop users who constantly travel store their email on their laptops in PST files because it's hard to keep synchronized with the corporate server while traveling.

Even so, if the email messages reside on an IMAP (Internet Message Access Protocol) or Exchange server, the deleted messages are harder for the end-user to permanently delete or destroy. However, once marked for deletion, the normal garbage collection process on the server is likely to recover space from deleted messages even more rapidly than if the email message is stored on the user's computer in a PST file — quickly making the message completely unrecoverable.

Some of the messages Senator Leahy is talking about were created and sent three or four years ago. If those messages were deleted years ago, it's entirely likely that many garbage collection cycles have occurred and those messages are long gone from servers.

Of course, that's why it's important to make regular backups and keep archival copies, but that's not what Senator Leahy is asserting here. Senator Leahy claims, "You can't erase emails, not today." Sadly, he's wrong. As I just showed you, email messages can be erased in a whole pile of different ways.

"They've gone through too many servers."

Without a doubt, email messages transit servers. In fact, the core architectural approach to email is a concept called Store and Forward. The idea is the server stores the message, then forwards it on to the next server in the chain. Unfortunately for Senator Leahy, the servers the messages travel through don't store the message any longer than it takes to move it to the next server.

There are archiving servers, specifically designed to hold email messages for further examination. We'll discuss archiving servers in a later chapter. But those systems have to be put into place in addition to the typical email server. It's not a normal function of email servers to hold mail messages in perpetuity after they've been forwarded. In fact, most servers, by design, don't hold those messages any longer than it takes to send them on, simply because the storage load would be overwhelming.

Again, sadly, the Senator is wrong.

"They can't say they've been lost."

Well, most Presidents say pretty much anything they darn well please. But the real statement here is the assertion that email messages can't be lost.

Sadly, they can.

Some years ago, I wrote an article called "My thirteen days in Exchange Hell" for *OutlookPower Magazine*. It's a story about how our Microsoft Exchange server's hard drive crashed. After constantly spinning at 7,200 revolutions per minute for three or four years in our overheated server closet, the drive's platters actually shattered into smithereens, as shown in Figure 3-1. We were unable to restore backups for almost two weeks. We'd done everything right, or so it seemed. We missed one critical element of the configuration puzzle and almost lost the entire company's email (including all our filed messages).

It took thirteen days and the support of some leading technology experts to recover our messages. We were finally able to do so. But when that hard drive crashed, if we didn't have a lot of backups (or if we had backups, but hadn't taken precautions to make image copies of the backups before attempting restores), we would have lost all those messages.

Yes, there are talented technicians who are really good at recovering lost email messages. But with a hard drive that physically shattered into dust, even the best forensic technician couldn't put Humpty Dumpty together again without a good set of backups.

So, sorry, Senator. Email messages can be lost.

Why this email thing is important

If you listen to the political press, you'd think the only reason anyone wanted those missing email messages was to dig through them to find something damning about the current administration and beat them up with it. And you'd probably be right.

It's really important to understand that, despite the politics, accurate email records are essential. They're important not just because the Presidential Records Act says they're important. They're important to those who sent the

Figure 3-1. *This is what the inside of the drive looked like. The platters were completely shattered. I'd never seen anything like it before in my life.*

messages, in case they need to go back and refer to a message they might have sent or received. They're important to history, so we, as a society, can go back years or decades later to understand intent and to better understand our leadership.

Perhaps more than anything else, those email messages are important because we have a new team in power every four to eight years. The new team may need to go back through the records to see what was promised, what decisions were made, the reasoning behind decisions, and the facts and observations used, so they can apply all that institutional knowledge to future decisions.

This is called "knowledge management" in the corporate world. Access to institutional knowledge is considered critical for business success and continuity. It's no less true when it comes to running a country.

Whether the next president is a Republican or Democrat, that institutional knowledge will be absolutely necessary, whether we're still prosecuting former officials — or still prosecuting a war.

Online resources

All of the links in this book are available from the book's Web site. Just visit *EmailsGone.com* and click on the Resources link. That way, you won't have to type in any long URLs.

Read the April 16 Press Briefing at *http://www.whitehouse.gov/news/ releases/2007/04/20070416-1.html*.

Read the Presidential Records Act at *http://www.archives.gov/about/laws/ presidential-records.html*.

Read the April 12th Press Briefing at *http://www.whitehouse.gov/news/ releases/2007/04/20070412-5.html*.

Read Senate Judiciary Commitee Chairman Patrick Leahy's statement in response to allegations of missing emails at *http://www.cnn.com/2007/ POLITICS/04/13/white.house.email/index.html*.

Read "My thirteen days in Exchange Hell" at *http://www.outlookpower.com/ issues/issue200410/00001297001.html*.

Tips from the ZATZ magazines

Some of the most common questions we get at *OutlookPower Magazine* are about PST files.

The most important thing to know about PST files is that their size is limited to 2 gigabytes for users of Outlook 2000 and earlier. Even users of Outlook 2003 and Outlook 2007 are limited to 20 gigabyte PST files.

To learn more about PST files, visit *http://www.OutlookPower.com* and type "PST" into the search box on the *OutlookPower* home page.

CHAPTER 4

Follow the domains

The whole White House email mess came to America's attention with the assertion that "potentially" millions of White House email messages have gone missing.

Politicians sometimes seem like rabid dogs. If there's anything that smells even vaguely like red meat, they attack with gusto. The late 2006 mid-term firing of eight United States Attorneys (and the subsequent controversy) provided our favorite Congress-critters with a great big mound of juicy, red meat.

As part of the poking and prodding that an opposing Congress does when it smells weakness in an administration, members of the 110th United States Congress discovered that many email messages sent by Karl Rove allegedly had not been archived — and therefore couldn't be examined for the purposes of the investigation into the firing of the U.S. Attorneys.

At the time, Mr. Rove was the Deputy White House Chief of Staff to U.S. President George W. Bush. He was also a political lightning-rod, widely considered Bush II's chief political strategist.

Although this book's investigation into White House email use is strictly technical in nature, I'll keep coming back to Mr. Rove throughout the book. That's because questions of his email usage proved to be the catalyst that got Congress going in their investigation — and details from that investigation have given me key clues that have helped me gain insight into how White House staffers use email.

As I discussed in the last chapter, there are possibly five million or more email messages missing, and they may include messages missing from government servers in addition to email messages missing from servers operated by the Republican National Committee.

My extended technical analysis has uncovered some concerns about unsecured email communications that might affect national security, transitions in server technology during a time of war that might have caused both communications interruptions and historical records loss, and data management practices that seriously question the technical email infrastructure being used by the Executive Office of the President.

The law behind it all

To understand why this is an issue, you must first understand a few laws that lay the groundwork for all the fuss. The Presidential Records Act of 1978, requires that:

> ...the activities, deliberations, decisions, and policies that reflect the performance of his constitutional, statutory, or other official or ceremonial duties are adequately documented and that such records are maintained as Presidential records...

Because the Act specifically defines "documentary material" to include correspondence and memorandums, and because the law also specifies "or other electronic or mechanical recordations," email messages sent or received as part of presidential business fall under the Presidential Records Act.

Bottom line: The administration is required to keep copies of all email.

The second law in question is the Hatch Act of 1939. Officially called "An Act to Prevent Pernicious Political Activities," the Hatch Act was originally put in place to prevent federal employees from joining an organization that wants to overthrow the government (it was big during the "red scare" of the 1950s).

Today, the Hatch Act allows Federal employees to participate in political parties, but prohibits them from engaging in political activity while on duty, in a government office, wearing an official uniform, or using a government vehicle.

Bottom line: You can't do political work while physically in the White House or using a government email account.

Karl Rove's email use

The issue that started Congress digging into White House email was, of course, what Karl Rove's involvement was in the firing of the Federal Attorneys. If he had involvement, his email was likely to shed some light on the extent of that involvement.

The desire to examine that email is what drove the investigation as a political issue. Actually, the irresistible desire get even with Mr. Rove for six years of political hardball is what drove a Democratically-controlled Congress into fits of investigatory delight, but the White House's poor email management practices gave them fuel to throw on the fire. Heck, if they were allowed to tar and feather the troublesome political operative, they'd do so.

Just as things started to get really exciting, when it looked like they might actually be able to make something stick to the guy, he resigned in August of 2007. Even though Rove's no longer Deputy Chief of Staff, his email and BlackBerry use while at the White House have helped me understand the flaws in the system — and so I'll be talking about him a lot within this book.

That said, Mr. Rove himself is not my concern. It's just that he's been such a main character in the Bush II White House saga that I can't really tell this story without including him in it.

Karl Rove apparently has at least two email accounts. The first is his official White House email account on *EOP.gov* (EOP meaning Executive Office of the President). The second is a political email address running on the domain *GWB43.com* (GWB43, of course, referring to George W. Bush, the 43rd President of the United States).

In the March 27th White House Press Briefing, Deputy Press Secretary Dana Perino stated:

> *What I know — I checked into this — is that certain White House officials and staff members who have responsibilities that straddle both worlds, that have responsibilities in communication, regular interface with political organizations, do have a separate email account for those political communications. That is entirely appropriate, especially when you think of it in this case, that the practice is in place and followed precisely to avoid any inadvertent violations of what is called the Hatch Act. And so there are some members of the administration that do straddle both worlds. And so under an abundance of caution so that they don't violate the Hatch Act, they have these separate emails.*

Bottom line: To keep politics off the government servers, Rove used the *GWB43.com* email account.

In the April 13 White House Press Gaggle, the following exchange indicated there might be more than these two accounts:

Q Okay, this is a quick two-parter. Karl Rove, I'm told, has multiple email accounts during this whole time at the White House, and he's conducted business over multiple accounts, not just two.

MS. PERINO: It's our understanding that those all funnel into one place.

Before we go on, let me make a note about formatting in this book. Whenever I quote something from a White House press briefing transcript, I always take the full format of the quote. The snippet shown above is a direct copy and paste of the actual briefing transcript. I left in the Q (without the colon) and the formatting of Ms. Perino's name (with the colon) for accuracy.

At the end of each chapter, I've provided a link to the full text of all the briefings we cite in that chapter. The *EmailsGone.com* site also has live links to the *WhiteHouse.gov* Web site where the briefings are located, as well as links to our own archive copies of the full briefings (in case they should someday vanish from the White House servers).

Technology in use

Let's spend a few minutes exploring what all this *EOP.gov* and *GWB43.com* stuff means. Both *EOP.gov* and *GWB43.com* are Internet domain names. You're likely to be familiar with other domain names, like *eBay.com, Amazon.com, Google.com,* and, of course, my company's own *ZATZ.com.* This book even has its own domain names. You can go to the book's Web site by typing in *WhereHaveAllTheEmailsGone.com,* or the much shorter variant *EmailsGone.com.*

Domain names serve a variety of purposes. They were initially designed to provide a memorable name for an Internet address, since it's much easier to remember *OutlookPower.com* than it is 63.254.227.203. As the Internet became more commercialized, domain names became brand names as well as mnemonic conveniences.

Both Web sites and email addresses use domain names, just in slightly different ways. To go to my company's Web site, you'd type *http://www.ZATZ.com* into a Web browser, but to send me an email message, you'd type *david@ZATZ.com* into the "To" field of your email message.

All this becomes important in our investigation because, internally to Internet operations, a domain name always leads to one or more physical computer servers. Once we knew the White House used the domains *EOP.gov* and *GWB43.com,* we were able to start digging. These domain names became our first clues.

Obviously, we don't have a detailed insight into exactly what technologies were being used *in toto*, both by Mr. Rove and by other members of the White House staff.

We do, however, have certain pieces of the puzzle, courtesy of Deputy Press Secretary Perino in her White House Press Gaggle of April 13. In specific, we know:

- The White House used Lotus Notes until 2002 or 2003.

- The White House currently uses Outlook.

- Mr. Rove and others also make heavy use of BlackBerry handheld devices.

We've never been able to explicitly confirm what server technologies were used, although we think it's fair to make a working assumption that the

Executive Office of the President used Lotus Domino until 2002 or 2003 and, most likely, Microsoft Exchange since then. That's because when most large organizations use Notes as an email client (the program people use), they also invariably use Lotus Domino as the server (the central program that runs everything). Likewise, when an organization uses Outlook as a client, it tends to use Exchange as a server. But we don't know for sure.

> **Question:** *What exact server technology is the Executive Office of the President using?*

Further, it's reasonable to assume that the BlackBerries in use by Mr. Rove and others probably run through a BlackBerry Enterprise Server. However, it's also important to realize that BlackBerry smartphones are also available from Internet service providers, phone companies, and even America Online, so we can't be sure Mr. Rove's and the other White House staffers' BlackBerry email traffic is or was traveling through an EOP-controlled server.

> **Question:** *What service is used to transmit White House political and official BlackBerry communications?*

We also don't know how Mr. Rove split up his EOP-related BlackBerry communication and his Republican National Committee-related BlackBerry communication although some testimony I'll cover later in the book provides some clues.

> **Question:** *Does Mr. Rove use more than one BlackBerry?*

Further, we can't really know what exact server technologies are being provided by the RNC (Republican National Committee) for the eighty-plus White House *GWB43.com* accounts. This is *very* important, because if they're using an Exchange server or even IMAP (Internet Message Access Protocol) server, saved messages would reside, at least for a while, on the server.

However, if they download their messages from the server via POP3 protocol to their personal computers or laptops, saved messages would reside solely on their local machines, in the .PST files we discussed in the last chapter.

> **Question:** *What protocol is used for GWB43.com email access?*

Finally, if Mr. Rove has other accounts beyond *EOP.gov* and *GWB43.com*, the same questions need to be asked. For example, if he has a Gmail account, much of his usage information is likely to be logged by Google and may be available as a result of a subpoena.

The next phase of our investigation

This is a huge story. In the next chapter, we'll look at the question of who runs *GWB43.com*, links from Karl Rove's email to Newt Gingrich, the Ohio GOP, and the strange question of whether Ohio's election results were run through a 12-person ISP in Chattanooga, Tennessee.

Online resources

All of the links in this book are available from the book's Web site. Just visit *EmailsGone.com* and click on the Resources link. That way, you won't have to type in any long URLs.

Read the Presidential Records Act of 1978 at *http://www.archives.gov/about/ laws/presidential-records.html.*

Read the Hatch Act at *http://www.osc.gov/ha_fed.htm.*

Read the March 27th Press Briefing at *http://www.whitehouse.gov/news/ releases/2007/03/20070327-4.html.*

Read the April 13 White House Press Gaggle *http://www.whitehouse.gov/news/ releases/2007/04/20070413-1.html.*

Tips from the ZATZ magazines

If you're interested in learning more about Lotus
Notes or Lotus Domino, check out *DominoPower
Magazine*.

DominoPower is the Web's largest independent
resource for IBM Lotus-related information,
knowledge, tips, and resources.

When you visit *DominoPower Magazine* (at
http://www.dominopower.com) you'll learn all
about IBM Lotus products and services and is all
about Lotus messaging and collaboration.

CHAPTER 5

Who runs GWB43.com?

In the previous chapter, we learned that the President's staff uses at least two domains for email: *EOP.gov* for official business and *GWB43.com* for political business. In this chapter, we'll explore *GWB43.com* for clues into the White House email infrastructure.

I've come up with some disturbing new questions.

Follow the domain

Like the good email geek I am, I did some research into the *GWB43.com* domain name, looking for whatever information I could find in the protocol wiring that runs deep under the surface of the Internet.

Finance guys follow the money. We geeks follow the domains.

Don't worry: if you're not a techie, you'll still understand most of what's in this chapter. A few items might be confusing, but stick with it. The end result is very interesting — and frankly, disturbing. By reading along, you'll get some exposure to how the Internet works "under the hood," which will help you understand more about a very important infrastructure on which we all rely.

As part of the investigative process, I grabbed "screenshots" of interesting online evidence. These screenshots are important, because they provide a snapshot of the information as I found it on the day I found it. Even if the Web sites change, you'll still be able to see a digital image of the site as it was.

Before I show you the first image from this investigation, it should be noted that I'm being quite rigorous in my editorial practices for this special investigation. Normally, in our online magazines, when we display an image in an article, we display a smaller thumbnail of the image, which links to a full image. That image may be very large, as has been the case for this investigation.

However, this is a printed book, not an online article. As such, you really can't go clicking these pages. Instead, I've included images in the book that showcase the most relevant information from the screenshot evidence I captured. If you want to see the full, complete image of what we captured, go to *EmailsGone.com,* and click on the Resources link. I have the full, large images linked to from there.

DNS basics

The DNS (Domain Name System) can be likened to a phone book for Internet communications. The DNS system is designed to translate human-understandable domain names (like *GWB43.com*) to Internet-understandable IP addresses (like 64.203.96.130) in much the same way that a phone book translates a person's name to his or her phone number.

These IP address translations are controlled at various levels by domain name servers. Most domains are controlled by specific DNSs. For example, all of our ZATZ domains are controlled by our own DNS servers, which are computers we own and operate, but are located in our ISP's highly-secured facility within the former Command and Control Center of what was once the Chanute Air Force Base, in a building affectionately known as "The Fortress."

Generally, a domain name like *GWB43.com* can lead you to a domain name server and (this is where it's interesting for our investigative purposes), a

Category	Status	Test Name	Information
Parent	PASS	Missing Direct Parent check	OK. Your direct parent zone exists, which is good. Some domains (usually third or fourth level domains, such as example.co.us) do not have a direct parent zone ('co.us' in this example), which is legal but can cause confusion.

	INFO	NS records at parent servers	Your NS records at the parent servers are:
			`a.ns.trespassers-w.net. [209.61.172.168] [TTL=172800] [US]`
			`ns1.cha.smartechcorp.net. [64.203.96.130] [TTL=172800] [US]`
			[These were obtained from d.gtld-servers.net]

	PASS	Parent nameservers have your nameservers listed	OK. When someone uses DNS to look up your domain, the first step (if it doesn't already know about your domain) is to go to the parent servers. If you aren't listed there, you can't be found. But you are listed there.
	PASS	Glue at parent nameservers	OK. The parent servers have glue for your nameservers. That means they send out the IP address of your nameservers, as well as their host names.
	PASS	DNS servers have A records	OK. All your DNS servers either have A records at the zone parent servers, or do not need them (if the DNS servers are on other TLDs). A records are required for your hostnames to ensure that other DNS servers can reach your DNS servers. Note that there will be problems if your DNS servers do not have these same A records.

DNS Report for gwb43.com

Generated by www.DNSreport.com at 08:04:52 GMT on 17 Apr 2007.

Figure 5-1. *Where does GWB43.com go?*

domain name server can lead you to the service provider managing the domain.

To get started, I first ran the DNS report shown in Figure 5-1 above.

Who runs GWB43.com?

It turns out that *GWB43.com* is managed by a domain name server located at *SMARTECHCORP.net* and another at the slightly creepy sounding (and possibly Winnie-the-Pooh-derived) *TRESPASSERS-W.net*. I wanted to confirm that *GWB43.com* was, in fact, the RNC (Republican National Committee) domain I'd seen discussed, so I also did a "whois" lookup on *GWB43.com*.

A whois lookup is the Internet's way of telling you who owns the domain. As Figure 5-2 shows, *GWB43.com* is owned by the RNC.

Figure 5-2. *GWB43.com is owned by the RNC.*

Figure 5-3. *RNCHQ.org also uses the same two domain name servers.*

Interestingly, the administrative and technical contacts for the *GWB43.com* domain are listed as an email address on the *RNCHQ.org* domain.

Finance guys follow the money. We geeks follow the domains.

So, who runs the *RNCHQ.org* domain? As you can see in Figure 5-3, the domain name servers are again *SMARTECHCORP.net* and *TRESPASSERS-W.net*.

Clearly, I've confirmed *SMARTECHCORP.net* and *TRESPASSERS-W.net* as operators of the RNC domains.

My next step was to find out who operates the *GWB43.com* email server.

What do we know about the GWB43.com mail server?

Email servers are identified to other email servers by what are called MX (or Mail Exchange) records. Each server that gets email has an MX record that's managed by the domain name server. So, my next step was to identify the MX record for *GWB43.com,* which I did, as shown in Figure 5-4.

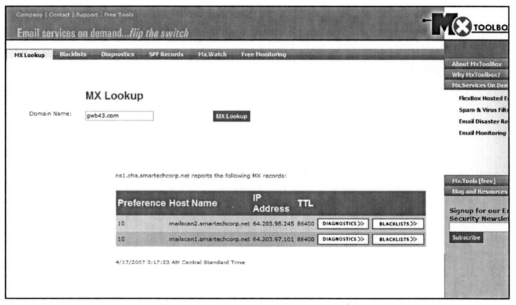

Figure 5-4. *Now we know where mail goes when it's sent to GWB43.com.*

Now we know where mail goes when it's sent to *GWB43.com.* It goes to one of two servers: *MAILSCAN1.SMARTECHCORP.net* and *MAILSCAN2.SMARTECHCORP.net.* So, once again, we bump into *SMARTECHCORP.net.*

Before we delve into further into *SMARTECHCORP.net* or the *GWB43.com* email server, it's important to understand some of the inherent limitations of my research. As you well know, email goes in and email goes out. The only thing public Internet records can show us is where a message first goes when it leaves an email client and it's headed for *GWB43.com*.

Whether the email lands at the first server, the publicly facing one according to the network records, or is stored and then forwarded on — this is something I can't see from the outside. So there's absolutely no way I can tell if Karl Rove or another member of the President's staff accessed incoming mail directly from these *SMARTECHCORP.net* servers.

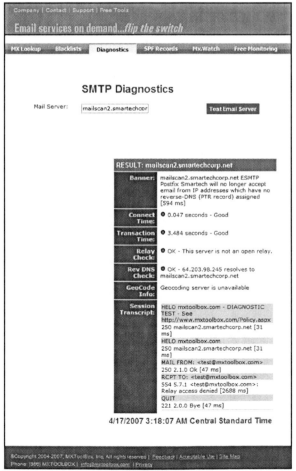

Likewise, if someone with a *GWB43.com* email address sends an email, that email might travel through the server I find, or it might go through a completely different path. I can't tell that solely from public records.

But we can find out a little more about *MAILSCAN1. SMARTECHCORP.net* and *MAILSCAN2. SMARTECHCORP.net*. Figure 5-5 shows an SMTP (Simple Mail Transport Protocol) session, connecting with *MAILSCAN1. SMARTECHCORP.net*.

Figure 5-5. *This is a Postfix server.*

The key piece of information is in the banner field of the session. The key word there is "Postfix," which is the name of a well-respected open-source email server program. We did a test on *MAILSCAN2.SMARTECHCORP.net* and got exactly the same results.

So now we know that when you send an email to someone on the *GWB43.com* domain, your email will travel to a Postfix server operated by *SMARTECHCORP.net.* So who is *SMARTECHCORP.net?*

In this next section, we'll look into SMARTech. In the next chapter, we'll take a very amusing look at *TRESSPASSERS-W.net.* the operators of the other DNS.

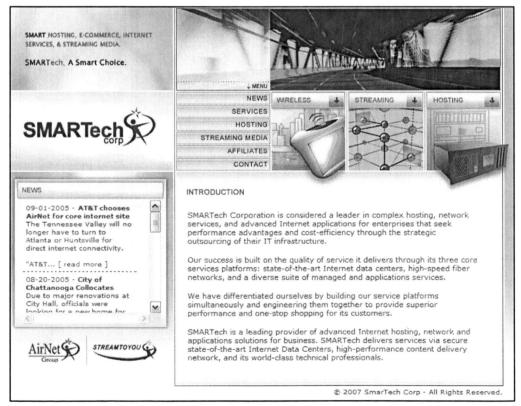

Figure 5-6. *Here's the home page for SMARTech Corporation.*

Understanding SMARTech Corporation

The easiest way to find something out about someone is when they make it publicly available. So we pointed our browsers to *http://www.smartechcorp.com* and did some reading. As Figure 5-6 shows, SMARTech Corporation is a small company located out of Chattanooga, Tennessee.

A page on their Web site states that SMARTech Corporation is owned by a Mr. Jeff Averbeck. The page indicates the company had 12 employees as of 2004 and also hosts *GEORGEWBUSH.com* and *GOP.com*.

```
42 domains sharing mailservers with gwb43.com
3edc.net
bcorker.com
bobcorkerforsenate.com
consultmhi.com
georgeallen.com
georgewbush.com
gingrichgroup.com
gingrichproductions.com
gop.com
gop.net
gop.org
gopcontact.com
gopcontact.org
gopemail.com
gopteamleader.com
govtechsolutions.com
newt.org
ohiogop.org
republicanvictoryteam.com
republicanvictoryteam.net
republicanvictoryteam.org
rga.org
rgppc.org
rnc.org
rncchairman.org
rnchq.org
rncmail.org
rslla.org
sharedhealth.com
socialsecurityblueprint.com
speakergingrich.com
```

In fact, Averbeck's SMARTech Corporation hosts a lot of GOP-related email and Web sites. We did a lookup to see what other domains seemed to run on the same mail server with *GWB43.com,* as shown in Figure 5-7.

In addition to the mail server domains we found, we found hundreds and hundreds domain names (including some fun ones like *ANGRYHILLARY.com* and *REAGANALUMNI.com*) operating on the SMARTech name servers.

Figure 5-7. *This screenshot shows some interesting domains on the same mail server.*

To get a full list, visit *EmailsGone.com* and click on the Resources link to see the complete data dump.

From the data dump, we can see that SMARTech also hosts mail on what appears to be the same server for a variety of domains, as shown in Table 5-1.

Table 5-1. *Email domains that appear to be hosted on the same server*

Domain(s)	Description
GEORGEALLEN.com	George Allen is the controversial former Republican Senator who lost his seat, in part, due to the use of a racial slur "macaca" in his campaign
BOBCORKER.com	Bob Corker is the junior U.S. Senator from Tennessee. He'll show up again, later in our story.
NEWT.org *SPEAKERGINGRICH.com* *SPEAKERGINGRICH.net* *SPEAKERGINGRICH.org* *GINGRICHGROUP.com* *GINGRICHPRODUCTIONS.com*	All are operated on behalf of Newt Gingrich, former Republican Speaker of the House.
GOP.com *GOPEMAIL.com* *REPUBLICANVICTORYTEAM.com* *RNC.org* *RNCMAIL.org* *RNCCHAIRMAN.org*	These are just a few of the GOP-related domains SMARTech seems to operate.
OHIOGOP.org	This is the Ohio Republican Party Web page. Ohio, of course, figured prominently in debates about the 2004 Presidential election.

Here at ZATZ, we use a neat little anti-phishing toolbar from Netcraft, a company that's been tracking hosting since the early days of the Internet. One of the useful things about Netcraft's toolbar is that it shows what ISP hosts the domain for a given server.

The Netcraft toolbar also helps you avoid "phishing," a nasty practice where unscrupulous Web site operators create fake Web sites that look like the ones you're used to, as a way of stealing your credit card and financial information.

If you're concerned about being "phished" (and you ought to be), the latest versions of both Microsoft Internet Explorer and Mozilla Firefox both include anti-phishing features. While not within the scope of this book, I've included some links at the end of this chapter about phishing, along with some ways you can protect yourself.

In any case, the Netcraft toolbar is a very easy way for us to see who actually physically "hosts" the servers belonging to a set of IP addresses. Figure 5-8 shows a comparison of the hosting ISP for our own *DominoPower Magazine* in the top half of the image with the hosting ISP for the SMARTech Corporation, shown in the bottom half.

As you can see, the toolbar shows that the fabulous Prominic.Net, Inc. is our ISP and SMARTECH CORPORATION is SMARTech's own ISP. This means

Figure 5-8. *It looks like SMARTech hosts their own servers.*

it's very likely SMARTech is running its own network feed and physically hosting its servers and Web sites at its own facility (rather than co-locating the machines at a bigger facility).

According to its "Contact Us" page, SMARTech is located at 801 Broad Street, Suite 220 in Chattanooga. Although I've had some very pleasant visits to Chattanooga, that was a long time ago. Fortunately, Google Earth can give us a bird's eye view of where SMARTech's servers seem to be located, as you can see in Figure 5-9. It doesn't exactly look like Fort Knox.

Figure 5-9. *The servers appear to be in downtown Chattanooga.*

But what else runs on the SMARTech servers? Netcraft can help here as well. I did a lookup on the netblock 64.203.96.0-64.203.111.255, which appear to be the IP addresses owned by SMARTech. Figure 5-10 shows all three pages returned by the Netcraft query.

SMARTech appears to mostly run Microsoft IIS and Apache servers. Digging through the sites operated by SMARTech, Table 5-2 shows more RNC-related customers, some local Chattanooga companies, and, strangely, at least one government Web site.

NETCRAFT

Toolbar	Netcraft

SMARTECH CORPORATION (page 1 of 3)

Rank	Site	Organisation	First Seen	Webserver	OS
5855919	campaignsolutions.com	Campaign Solutions, 118 North Saint Asaph Street, Alexandria, 22314, United States	April 2000	Apache/1.3.33 (Unix) mod_jk/1.2.6 PHP/4.3.10 mod_ssl/2.8.22 OpenSSL/0.9.7d	FreeBSD
-	e49.com	episode49, LLC	May 2005	Microsoft-IIS/6.0	Windows Server 2003
3655848	georgebush.com	Bush-Cheney '04, Inc., P.O. Box 10648, Arlington, 22210, United States	April 2000	Microsoft-IIS/6.0	Windows Server 2003
353216	gop.com	Republican National Committee, 310 First Street SE, Washington, 20003, United States	March 2002	Microsoft-IIS/6.0	Windows Server 2003
-	govtechsolutions.com	Govtech Solutions, 1133 21st Street, Suite M 100, Washington, 20036, United States	June 2000	Microsoft-IIS/6.0	Windows Server 2003
1349700	johnmccain.com	Domains by Proxy, Inc., 15111 N. Hayden Rd., Ste 160, PMB 353, Scottsdale, Arizona 85260, United States, Registered through: GoDaddy.com, India	May 1998	Microsoft-IIS/6.0	Windows Server 2003
-	mail.nationalposters.com	National Posters, 2464 Amnicola Highway, Chattanooga, 37406, United States	November 2002	Apache/1.3.32 (Unix) DAV/1.0.3 mod_perl/1.29 PHP/5.1.4	FreeBSD
-	mail.youmagonline.com	Mcdonald, David, True North Custom Publishing, P.O. Box 4449, Chattanooga, 37405, United States	unknown	Apache/1.3.33 (Unix) mod_perl/1.29 PHP/4.3.10	FreeBSD
1031245	media1.streamtoyou.com	Smartech Corporation, Smartech Corporation (NA), Null, Po Box 11181, Chattanooga, 37401-2181, United States	July 2003	Cougar/9.01.01.3814	Windows Server 2003
865536	newt.org	Whois Privacy Protection Service, Inc., PMB 368, 14150 NE 20th St - F1, Bellevue, 98007, United States	March 2000	Microsoft-IIS/6.0	Windows Server 2003

Figure 5-10. *SMARTech appears to run Microsoft IIS and Apache servers.*

Table 5-2. *Some Web sites that can be located in SMARTech's IP address block*

Domain	Description
JOHNMCCAIN.com	John McCain, of course, is the once leading contender in the 2008 Presidential race. He's had the domain operating since 1998.
RPTF.com	This is the National Republican Senatorial Committee
OFHEO.gov	This is the Web site for the Office of Federal Housing Enterprise Oversight, part of Housing and Urban Development. According to Wikipedia, "It is charged with ensuring the capital adequacy and financial safety and soundness of two government sponsored enterprises — the Federal National Mortgage Association (Fannie Mae) and the Federal Home Loan Mortgage Corporation (Freddie Mac)."

So, what else can we find out about SMARTech and Jeff Averbeck?

According to *CampaignMoney.com,* Averbeck donated a total of $5,320 to the RNC between 2000 and 2006. According to Federal Election Commission records, the RNC purchased Web services from SMARTech:

- $15,213.06 on 12/17/2003
- $15,213.06 on 12/18/2003
- $819.38 on 12/23/2003

The RNC also purchased Web services, from Airnet Group, Inc. (which is the name of the company that owns SMARTech):

- $14,884.31 on 10/02/2003
- $1,365.63 on 11/06/2003

In total, it looks like the RNC spent $47,495.44 back in 2003 with Averbeck's company to set up and manage Web sites. On the surface, that may look like a lot of money but, as someone who's managed Web sites and bought high-speed Internet feeds, I can assure you that's actually a pretty reasonable price to run such high-profile Web sites.

It should be noted that I offered Mr. Averbeck the opportunity to comment on our coverage and answer interview questions. In fact, I promised him I'd ask him questions via email and publish his written answers, in full and completely unedited. Although I left Mr. Averbeck a detailed message with this promise in his personal voice mailbox, the call was never returned — the offer still stands should he read this and wish to comment.

Strange assertions about Ohio election results

Once you start turning over rocks, you never know what you might discover. Without a doubt, tracing electronic records from any political party is going to turn over a *lot* of controversial claims. The weirdest relates to the Ohio elections and SMARTech.

We independently established earlier that *OHIOGOP.org* was operated by SMARTech. However, there are claims that Ohio's official election sites for the mid-term 2006 elections were outsourced to SMARTech as well. The (very) liberal Web site ePluribus Media claims that:

> *The State of Ohio's real-time, streaming election results are first diverted through Chattanooga, TN, to a GOP-only web firm and the servers currently hosting georgewbush.com, as well as other key Republican web sites.*

They claim that *ELECTION.SOS.STATE.OH.US* was routed to a SMARTech server. This is interesting because Ohio's then Secretary of State (the person who oversees Ohio's elections) was a Republican named Ken Blackwell. Mr. Blackwell was running for Governor of Ohio.

Mr. Blackwell served under the first President Bush as undersecretary of Department of Housing and Urban Development (remember, we earlier saw another HUD agency running its Web site through SMARTech). President Bush (senior) later appointed Blackwell as ambassador to the United Nations Human Rights Commission. Blackwell served in that post from 1992 to 1993.

If the state's election information page was re-routed from a government server to a server located at SMARTech, then why? Does that mean something's not entirely kosher?

Sadly, our source here is anything but objective. So we can't accept ePluribus' rant as independent information. I did, however, do some research on my own. Their claim is that Ohio hosted election information on IP address 64.203.98.137. A quick "whois" search confirms that SMARTech does indeed own that IP address, as shown in Figure 5-11.

In fact, as I showed earlier, they appear to own 64.203.96.0 through 64.203.111.255. Owning a block of IP addresses isn't unusual for a firm that does Web hosting and provides other Internet services, so there's nothing troubling here. What is unusual is that SMARTech does appear have hosted at least some information from the Office of the Ohio Secretary of State, as shown in Figure 5-12.

I have no idependent verification of any of the primary assertions from ePluribus. It is, however, curious that official state election documents do appear on a server operated by a firm

```
Output from ARIN WHOIS

ARIN Home Page    ARIN Site Map    ARIN WHOIS Help    Tutorial on Querying ARIN's WHOIS

Search for : [                    ]  Submit Query

Search results for: 64.203.98.137


    OrgName:      SMARTECH CORPORATION
    OrgID:        SCOR
    Address:      PO BOX 11161
    City:         Chattanooga
    StateProv:    TN
    PostalCode:   37401
    Country:      US

    NetRange:     64.203.96.0 - 64.203.111.255
    CIDR:         64.203.96.0/20
    NetName:      SMARTECHCORPNET
    NetHandle:    NET-64-203-96-0-1
    Parent:       NET-64-0-0-0-0
    NetType:      Direct Allocation
    NameServer:   NS1.CHA.SMARTECHCORP.NET
    NameServer:   A.NS.TRESPASSERS-W.NET
    Comment:
    RegDate:      2004-01-15
    Updated:      2004-01-15

    RAbuseHandle: ABUSE152-ARIN
    RAbuseName:   Abuse Group
    RAbusePhone:  +1-423-664-7678
    RAbuseEmail:  abuse@smartechcorp.net

    RTechHandle:  AG865-ARIN
    RTechName:    Garrison, Alvin
    RTechPhone:   +1-423-664-7678
    RTechEmail:   noc@smartechcorp.net

    OrgAbuseHandle: ABUSE152-ARIN
    OrgAbuseName:   Abuse Group
    OrgAbusePhone:  +1-423-664-7678
    OrgAbuseEmail:  abuse@smartechcorp.net

    OrgTechHandle:  AG865-ARIN
    OrgTechName:    Garrison, Alvin
    OrgTechPhone:   +1-423-664-7678
    OrgTechEmail:   noc@smartechcorp.net

    # ARIN WHOIS database, last updated 2007-04-18 19:10
    # Enter ? for additional hints on searching ARIN's WHOIS database.

If contact information is out of date or incorrect, please contact hostmaster@arin.net.
```

Figure 5-11. *SMARTech does own the IP address.*

Figure 5-12. *SMARTech is hosting some official Ohio election documents.*

under contract to the RNC. It is also curious that the senior election official in Ohio was also running for Governor of Ohio while this went on. It is further somewhat curious that a finance oversight agency of HUD runs its Web site on SMARTech's servers and that Mr. Blackwell was previously undersecretary of HUD. Nothing of this, however, represents anything even close to a smoking gun.

Mr. Blackwell was defeated in the election.

Introducing "Deep Mail"

Anyone with even the slightest understanding of recent American history has heard of Deep Throat (now known to be former FBI second-in-command William Mark Felt, Sr.).

Felt (a.k.a. Deep Throat) provided insider information and clues to *Washington Post* investigative journalists Bob Woodward and Carl Bernstein during their initial investigation of Watergate back in the early 1970s.

It appears we may have our own Deep Throat on our hands. After we originally published the information from this chapter in *OutlookPower Magazine* and *DominoPower Magazine,* I got some interesting email from someone with a very anonymous Google Gmail account.

I sent him (or her) back an email, asking for some clarification and specifically asking who he is. The person identified himself as "...one of the researchers with ePluribus Media" and signed his name simply as "Intranets".

This being just too juicy to pass up, we've decided to nickname him "Deep Mail" and publish the information he provided us. His complete letters to us are contained in Appendix A.

I haven't verified anything Deep Mail has reported in his letters nor do I know who he is (or even if he really is a "he"). Deep Mail continued to send us smaller comments from time-to-time as our coverage continued. You'll need to use your own judgement as to what you think about his comments.

Why SMARTech?

This brings us back to the email management issue that got us started. In addition to running Postfix, it's reasonable to assume that SMARTech runs Microsoft's Exchange server and other Microsoft technology. As Figure 5-13 shows, Averbeck is quoted by Microsoft as endorsing Microsoft's Small Business Server.

From this, and because we know SMARTech runs the open source Apache and Microsoft's IIS and Windows Server 2003, we can reasonably guess the

Figure 5-13. *Back in 1999, Averbeck endorsed Microsoft technology.*

RNC email servers use either Postfix or Exchange (or both). But this begs a far bigger question.

> **Question:** *Why would the RNC run so much critical information through a tiny 12-person ISP in Chattanooga?*

Conspiracy theorists could go to town over this question, but I'd caution restraint. When faced with deciding between a vast global conspiracy or someone's inherent lack of knowledge, lack of knowledge wins almost every time. Face it: wouldn't you rather give a project you don't understand to someone you trust than a huge company you can't influence?

I've had that experience. We've run our Internet services through huge companies and small companies. For years, we used Verizon to provide us with an Internet feed. It was an exercise in constant frustration.

For the past few years, we've run our Internet services through a small company (probably about the size of SMARTech) called Prominic.NET. Working with Prominic has been a total joy. Responsiveness, knowledge, and customer service are so vastly better with Prominic than Verizon that it's almost indescribable.

When faced with deciding who to have help implement their Internet needs, I'm sure the head honchos at the RNC weren't familiar with SMTP, POP, SSH, and all the other "geekspeak" terms we use every day.

This brings me back to Chattanooga's former Mayor and newly minted Republican Senator Bob Corker. As an Associated Press article shows, Corker knew SMARTech's Averbeck. I think it's likely that Averbeck connected with the RNC due to his connections with Corker.

Based on my examination of the coding of the SMARTech Web site, the lack of errors in SMARTech's DNS, MX, and IP setup I found during my investigation, and Microsoft's use of his endorsement for Small Business Server, it's likely Mr. Averbeck knows his stuff.

So, which is more likely? Vast right-wing conspiracy or "I know a guy?" Personally, I'd bet on the "I know a guy" factor every time.

But just because we don't see a conspiracy here doesn't mean we don't see a troublesome national security risk. In the next chapter, we'll continue our detailed analysis, look into the strange TRESPASSERS-W story, and we'll share with you some of our ongoing security concerns.

Online resources

All of the links in this book are available from the book's Web site. Just visit *EmailsGone.com* and click on the Resources link. That way, you won't have to type in any long URLs.

Visit Prominic.NET at *http://www.prominic.net*.

Visit SMARTech Corporation at *http://www.smartechcorp.com*.

Get the Netcraft toolbar at *http://toolbar.netcraft.com*.

Read the CampaignMoney.com data on Averbeck at *http://www.campaignmoney.com/political/contributions/jeff-averbeck.asp?cycle=04*.

Read Federal Election Commission records at *http://herndon2.sdrdc.com/cgi-bin/dcdev/forms/C00386987/150115/sb/ALL/5*.

Read further Federal Election Commission records at *http://herndon2.sdrdc.com/cgi-bin/dcdev/forms/C00386987/150115/sb/ALL/3*.

Visit ePluribus Media's story at *http://scoop.epluribusmedia.org/story/2006/11/7/115314/922*.

Read the Associated Press article on SMARTech at *http://www.airnetgroup.com/index.php?s=news&n=6*.

Visit the Airnet Group at *http://www.airnetgroup.com*.

Tips from the ZATZ magazines

If you're concerned about "phishing," I recommend two important articles.

The first, in *OutlookPower,* is "Defend yourself from phishing," at *http://www.outlookpower.com/issues/issue200702/00001939001.html.*

The second, also from *OutlookPower Magazine,* is "There's a scammer born every day," at *http://www.outlookpower.com/issues/issue200509/00001641001.html.*

CHAPTER 6

A detour into mob journalism

For the past few chapters, I've been conducting a detailed, in-depth technical analysis of the White House missing email controversy. Because very little information was easily available, I've had to take each step in sequence and carefully document my observations.

I found some amazingly immature behavior from a bunch of geeks.

Earlier, in Chapter 4, we learned that the President's staff uses at least two domains for email: *EOP.gov* for official business and *GWB43.com* for political business. In Chapter 5, we explored *GWB43.com* for clues into the White House email infrastructure and came up with some disturbing questions. In this chapter, I take a strange detour into what I call "mob journalism" as I continue to dig for the truth.

It should be noted that here at ZATZ we've thought very carefully about whether we should be covering this story. Even though our coverage is completely technical in nature, it does touch on political issues since I'm looking at the email practices of a sitting President's administration.

Not only have I discovered a national security concern about email management, but I've also identified and will, in later chapters, discuss a serious systemic concern in how the United States Government treats email. This is not a red state/blue state issue or even one of Republicans vs. Democrats. If you recall, I talked about similar email management problems in the Clinton administration back in Chapter 2.

Instead, this is about how non-technical people are relying almost totally on a technical solution they don't fully understand — and how that lack of understanding could cause serious security failures for the United States government. Further, since most other national governments likely rely on email within their infrastructure, this book has lessons for national leaders and their advisors outside the United States, as well.

This isn't about whether you like George W. Bush or not, or whether you liked Bill Clinton or not. It's about email usage, management and oversight in the Executive Office of the President — not just George W. Bush's EOP, but email usage for any administration.

And with that, we continue our tour throught the digital detritus of the White House email system.

The road, thus far

In this chapter, I'll continue looking into the DNS records for *GWB43.com*. In the previous chapter, I answered the question "Who runs *GWB43.com*?" with the identification of SMARTech Corporation as the company that provided domain name services, email services, and Web services for many Republican candidates, campaigns, and government officials.

Even though there was a very curious question of why some podunk ISP in the middle of Tennessee was used as the primary gateway for Republican digital politics and a very weird link between the Republican Ohio gubernatorial candidate who also oversaw the Ohio elections and SMARTech, I found no evidence of wrongdoing with SMARTech.

However, the secondary DNS for *GWB43.com* is provided by one *TRESPASSERS-W.net,* as I showed in the last chapter, in Figure 5-1.

In this chapter, we'll look into the very weird story of *TRESPASSERS-W.net.* I didn't find anything suspect from the point of view of my investigation into possible missing email messages, but I did find some amazingly immature behavior from a bunch of geeks.

Trespassing on TRESPASSERS-W

As with my previous investigation into SMARTech, I began my look at *TRESPASSERS-W.net* with a "whois" lookup on *TRESPASSERS-W.net,* as shown in Figure 6-1.

As the report shows, *TRESPASSERS-W.net* appears to be operated by Jeffrey Cross, who is listed as the registrant with Cross Computer Consulting (at *CROSS-CC.com*) and with Coptix Inc. (at *COPTIX.net).* Coptix, it turns out, is a Web development firm, also located in Chattanooga.

Figure 6-1. *Whois TRESPASSERS-W.net?*

Like I did with the MX records in the last chapter, I looked for further information on these two companies. As far as I can tell, the only independently provable digital link between *TRESPASSERS-W.net* and the Executive Office of the President is that TRESPASSERS-W is a secondary DNS for *GWB43.com*.

But, when I did a search on "Coptix," also listed in the whois data dump, I found a whole host of references to Karl Rove. And a *very* silly story.

Coptix cops to a digital chop

As anyone with any visible presence online can attest to, the so-called "blogosphere" can be a pretty cruel place. You've no doubt heard of blogs, a form of citizen journalism where anyone with an Internet connection and eight bucks a month can publish their most personal thoughts.

To be fair, there are some amazingly talented bloggers out there, commenting, educating, creating, and conducting solid journalism. There are also a whole lot of them who simply seem to exist to rain on other people's parade. Pretty much whenever you get a large mass of humanity together, you're going to get some spoil-sports.

I've certainly gotten my unfair share of digital badmouthing. While some incredible journalism can and does take place on blogs, there's also a whole lot of judgement, shoot-from-the-hip reporting, and vitriolic opinion bubbling up from the bowels of blogs.

Here at ZATZ, we're not the first to look into the White House email controversy, although it seems we're doing the most comprehensive analysis and we're most definitely one of the few publishers without a partisan axe to grind. Plus, with deep experience covering Notes and Domino, as well as mobile devices, we're probably the most technically qualified to cover the topic.

Apparently, a bunch of folks with a definite partisan bent found out the same thing I did: that Coptix runs a DNS server for *GWB43.com*.

And then, Mr. Cross and the Coptix team sat back and waited for the blogosphere to blow a gasket. Which, in short order, it did.

However, they were far less kind about their discovery. These bloggers made the unsupported assumption that just because *GWB43.com* exists, its mere

 existence implies that "all" White House email was routed through it.

The bloggers then took the next unsupported leap, claiming that those operating the servers were obviously hiding the White House email messages.

Figure 6-2. *Karl's porking up at Porker's.*

Apparently, this did not sit well with Cross and the techies of Coptix. They got their hands on an image of Karl Rove in Porker's Bar-B-Que in Chattanooga, as shown in Figure 6-2.

Then, the boys at Coptix fired up Photoshop, updating the image to show Mr. Rove holding a report with Coptix' name on the front, as shown in Figure 6-3.

Photoshop, of
course, is the
amazing image
retouching
program used
by artists,
photographers,
and graphic
professionals to
transform images
into anything
they might want.

While
Photoshop is an

Figure 6-3. *Mr. Rove is apparently holding a Coptix report.*

excellent tool for photographers, it is often so good that it's capable of taking
a photograph and modifying it in such a way that you can't tell what was
originally in view and what's been added by the photographic artist.

As I'll show a little later in this chapter, the Coptix kids did a passable
job at retouching the image to add in what appears to be a Coptix report.
Photographic analysis shows, however, they missed a few spots.

Once they published the modified photo on the Web, Mr. Cross and the
Coptix team sat back and waited for the blogosphere to blow a gasket. Which,
in short order, it did.

One such example of unresearched gasket-blowing was Corrente, a blog which
self-identifies as "Boldly shrill."

I'm not exactly sure that being "boldly shrill" is something you'd want to brag about but, in any case, Corrente said this about Coptix:

> *Karl went out and hired his own, bespoke, politically wired nameserver company. Of course, Karl would never give business to any company that hadn't sworn fealty to the authoritarian agenda, but I imagine Karl is also getting a level of, erm, personal service that he wouldn't get from a fiddy-dollar administrator like GoDaddy or Yahoo or whatever.*

and...

> *Nameserver administrators also provide email forwarding, which is the equivalent of call-forwarding on the Intertubes. So, if Karl wanted to store all his email safely offshore in, oh, American Samoa or Guam, then Coptix would be the company to do that for him.*

A Washington, D.C. gossip blog, Wonkette, called Coptix "GOP stooges" and then went on to say:

> *The White House illegally routes the administration's criminal email through a private Internet Web server in a clumsy yet still illegal attempt to keep the Crime Organization's communications out of the public eye.*

Yowch! Not exactly objective coverage, that. And, sadly, it's also wrong. I'll discuss the issue of routing email through SMARTech throughout this book, but while it's a flawed practice, I've found nothing to indicate the practice is illegal. Plus, I found no evidence that RNC email was ever sent via Coptix.

Traffic all across the Internet jumped to judgement, claiming that because Mr. Rove had a document in his hands from an Internet company, he was "privatizing" his White House email in an effort to hide it from public view.

Shortly after this story exploded, Josiah Roe, Executive Vice President of Coptix Inc. published an explanation in the Chattanooga Times Free Press:

> *Our experiment demonstrated that, as with all great marketing, Web marketing can be used by a few people to shape the way that millions think. Of course, we ran our test on April Fool's weekend, when bloggers, like all journalists, should have their skepticism synapses at their sharpest. Today, two very busy days later, we are reminded that the Internet is a tool to be mastered rather than feared, and that the right word whispered in the right ear can still carry around the world.*

If you're going to doctor a photo, don't forget the shadows

Here at ZATZ, we also publish *Connected Photographer Magazine*, which we bill as "Not your typical photo magazine." *Connected Photographer* is all about the art, science, and joy of making a connection through photographs in the Internet Age.

If you're not familiar with Sleestaks, perhaps you're just not geeky enough.

While doing my original detailed forensic analysis of the White House email controversy, I bumped into the very strange Coptix story that has a doctored photo at its core. That made it fair game for us to play with in *Connected Photographer,* especially since we figured readers would get a kick out of the wacky photo retouching aspect of it.

This book is, of course, dedicated to understanding problems with White House email. Even so, this little detour should appeal to any of you who are digital photographers and those with a twisted sense of humor.

Figure 6-4. *There be Sleestaks here.*

Just in case you can't get enough of the whole lizard people *meme* that so often appears in popular culture, in the next few pages, we'll also take a closer look at the retouching itself — and an interesting mistake.

Examining the hacked images

You can see the changes between the two images more clearly in Figure 6-4.

Not only was the Coptix report placed under Mr. Rove's arm, but the television image was changed as well. Instead of the woman in the original picture, our intrepid team of photo retouchers inserted a picture of Sleestaks.

If you're not familiar with Sleestaks, perhaps you're just not geeky enough. For those of you who aren't intimately familiar with 1970's cult scifi, the Sleestaks are large, green reptilian/insectoid hybrid creatures (basically, lizard people) that were featured in the 1974 series *Land of the Lost.* Apparently, the Coptix kids had a lot of time on their hands.

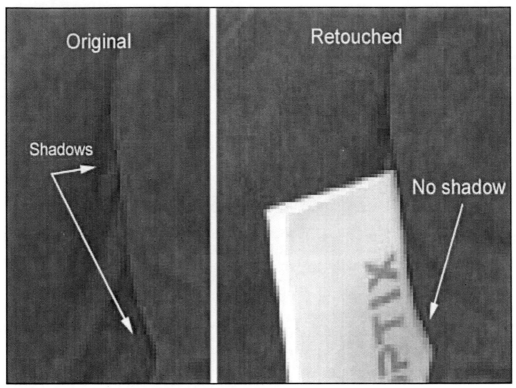

Figure 6-5. *There's no shadow on the report.*

While the Sleestak image clearly was a gag, the report under Mr. Rove's arm was obviously meant to send a message. Although placement of the report in the image is pretty well done (thanks to Photoshop), there's one "gotcha" visible from the enlarged image shown in Figure 6-5.

As you can see, on the left side, under Mr. Rove's sleeve, there's a shadow. On the retouched side, where the report was placed, even though there's a gap between the sleeve and the report, there's no shadow.

It was a nice job, nonetheless.

I'd ordinarily like to end a discussion like this with a deep, insightful conclusion and I will, further down on this page. Here, though, rather than looking deeply into issues of journalistic integrity, I'm simply going to recommend that if you retouch images, keep track of your shadows.

Moving on

While the bulk of this investigative report into White House email is intended to be technical in nature, I've found all sorts of interesting detours along the way. There's no evidence that Coptix is anything more than they seem — Web developers with a twisted sense of humor and outrage.

Citizen journalism is a very powerful thing. Matt Drudge single-handedly opened the door to the Bill Clinton/Monica Lewinsky scandal. In the past decade, digital journalism has scooped traditional "mainstream media" over and over again with exceptional reporting and detailed analysis.

But blogging and citizen journalism also has a darker side, a mob mentality. Many of the so-called "first tier" blogs tend to rush to judgement, triggering an avalanche of follow-on pile-on from hundreds of other bloggers.

The Coptix case is a perfect example. There really is a story in the missing White House email messages. And, as I've shown throughout this book, it has freaky national security consequences. But because of the blogger pile-on effect, the virtual equivalent of crying wolf, it may be harder to find the truth among all the unsupported claims.

For us here at ZATZ, doing our best to conduct objective journalism, it gets just a bit harder. As I looked further into the questions surrounding the White House email debate, I found that I couldn't reliably accept blog or mainstream media reports as valid sources.

And that's why, you may have noticed, I've gone straight to the actual source. Rather than quoting newspapers quoting press briefings at the White House, I'm giving you links to the actual briefings. The same is true of Congressional testimony, where I'll provide you with links to the official transcripts.

I continue to look into this case throughout the book. But I am going to do my absolute best to give you access to the original sources I've found, so you can do your own analysis as well.

Hopefully, we'll be able to avoid more childish detours into mob journalism.

Online resources

All of the links in this book are available from the book's Web site. Just visit *EmailsGone.com* and click on the Resources link. That way, you won't have to type in any long URLs.

Read the Corrente rant at *http://www.correntewire.com/rove_spotted_in_ chattanooga_with_brochure_for_gwb43_com_nameserver_host_can_we_ subpoena_the_records_now.*

Read Wonkette's take on the story at *http://wonkette.com/politics/karl-rove/ gop-stooges-now-claim-sleestak+rove+coptix-picture-is-fake-249458.php.*

Read the Coptix explanation in the Chattanooga Times Free Press at *http://www.timesfreepress.com/absolutenm/templates/blog-1. aspx?articleid=13342&zoneid=11.*

CHAPTER 7

The nightmare scenario

Back in World War II, the Allies made enormous advances against Hitler's forces, in part because of an extreme effort to crack the encryption used by the Nazis. The codebreaking efforts done at England's Bletchley Park, especially the cracking of the Enigma code, are widely credited with shortening the war.

Despite all the efforts of our modern-day United States military and security establishments to keep America's own plans secure and secret, all of that work could potentially be undone simply because our nation's most senior leaders are forced, by law, to use non-government systems for communicating anything with an even remotely political element.

The problem is not our vastly superior security and encryption technology. The problem is that all of that technology is simply not being used.

Since much of what goes on in any White House is political by nature, the Hatch Act forces our leadership to completely bypass the best the American security establishment can offer for much of their communication. Instead, our leaders are forced to rely on the efforts of a 12-person ISP in Chattanooga — and the open, unsecured, globally accessible Internet for sending email.

It took the Allies 10,000 people working 24/7 at Bletchley Park to crack Enigma. The encyption and security technology we have today is vastly superior. The United States National Security Agency has most of the top encryption and code-cracking scientists in the world working for it. But the problem isn't our vastly superior security and encryption technology. The problem is that all of that technology is simply not being used.

Remember, the Hatch Act explicitly states that government resources can't be used for political discussions. So all the wildly powerful technology at the disposal of the United States government, must, by law, remain unused by our nation's leaders for any communication that, in any way, may have a political component.

> **Question:** *How many White House staffers are just "defaulting" to sending all their email out via their political accounts so that they don't inadvertently slip up and violate the Hatch Act?*

Estimating a wildly conservative figure of 50 pieces of email a day per staffer, we're talking 18 million messages or more, each year, completely open and available for our enemies to read. In the 2,072 days between September 11, 2001 and May 15, 2007, a minimum of 103.6 million messages have likely been sent by White House staffers, completely in the open, for anyone to read.

And that's a nightmare scenario.

I alluded to the potentially nightmarish national security implications of this practice in Chapter 1. In this chapter, we'll explore, in-depth, the technical details of what makes this is so troubling.

Quick recap

Let's do a quick recap first. The Hatch Act says that government workers can't use government facilities to engage in political activities. As a key political advisor, White House Deputy Chief of Staff Karl Rove was subject to the Hatch Act and when he wanted to send email messages of a political nature, the law required him to use non-government systems to do so.

Although Mr. Rove has since resigned his position, much of what we know of White House email operations came from White House press briefings about his involvement with the missing email scandal and from Congressional testimony investigating it. Therefore, it's instructive to look at how he used these systems and extrapolate from that how others in the White House continue to use them.

In the 2,072 days between September 11, 2001 and May 15, 2007, a minimum of 103.6 million messages have likely been sent by White House staffers, completely in the open, for anyone to read.

The non-government systems he used appear to be servers operated by SMARTech Corporation, a 12-person ISP located in Chattanooga, Tennessee. We know that that SMARTech operates a Postfix email server (a well-respected open source email server).

Due to evidence showing SMARTech's Jeff Averbeck appearing in a Microsoft press release, it's also likely that SMARTech operates a Microsoft Exchange server, but that's really just educated speculation. We have no way to speculate about what kind of encryption technology SMARTech may or may not be using.

> **Question:** *What, if any, encryption technology is in place to protect important government email sent from political party accounts?*

In the April 13, 2007 Press Gaggle, White House Acting Press Secretary Dana Perino confirmed that White House staffers use Outlook and BlackBerry handhelds.

Educated guesses

At this point, it's important to be clear that I don't have a lot of tangible information on the full spectrum of email clients and servers used. In fact, I probably have less evidentiary information for this chapter than for any other chapter in this book.

However, speaking not entirely immodestly, I do know a bit about email. Most of the educated guesses I'm going to make throughout this article can be backed up by my relatively deep understanding of email usage patterns.

And that brings us back to Mr. Rove, White House staffers like him, and how they use email at the White House.

What we can't really be sure of is whether White House staffers like Mr. Rove use Outlook and BlackBerry handhelds for official government business, Republican political business, or both.

> **Question:** *Did Mr. Rove and other staffers use Outlook and BlackBerry handhelds for official government business, Republican political business, or both?*

I think it's a fair bet to assume that Mr. Rove used Outlook and his BlackBerry for both, simply because switching between email clients is likely to be a pain in daily use.

Earlier in my research, I looked into whether Mr. Rove used other email accounts as well, in particular accounts like Google's Gmail and Microsoft's Hotmail. Because I don't have access to any confirmed answers and because I've found no evidence — or even wild-eyed blog claims — of Web-based email usage, I'm going to ignore that possible aspect of his email usage unless something new surfaces. I did find some Congressional testimony indicating he also has an America Online account, but not what he uses it for.

In this chapter, I'm going to look at how a White House staffer would send a message from Outlook, get a message into Outlook, and do the same with a BlackBerry.

I also have no specific mention of Microsoft Exchange as an email server for either the RNC or EOP. But I think it's a reasonable probability that both the RNC and EOP use Exchange, given Mr. Rove and other staffers' active use of the BlackBerry handheld smartphone. Here's why.

Generally, there are two basic email management paradigms: either email messages live on the server or email messages get downloaded to the client (running on a user's personal computer). Once you download email messages to a client, usually through the POP3 protocol, your messages exist solely on the client and can't be easily shared among machines.

If you're using a BlackBerry, however, it's unlikely you'll want to download all your email messages just to the BlackBerry. It's far more likely you'll want to keep your email messages on the server so you can reference them from any client you use, whether your BlackBerry or your Outlook client on your desktop or laptop computer.

Understanding the BlackBerry component

To get a better understanding of where the BlackBerry handheld fits in, I decided to bring in an expert. I had the opportunity to get some security information from Gary Morse, president of Razorpoint Security. Gary is a professional "white hat" hacker who specializes in network security.

Gary has more than 20 years experience in information technology, focusing on security, network architecture and new media. In particular, he is an expert in attack/penetration testing, which uncovers and identifies vulnerabilities used by hackers against corporate networks.

Gary's been interviewed by CNN, CNBC, the New York Times, Forbes, Court TV, and other well-respected media outlets and he's our "go to guy" for BlackBerry security info. What follows is a short Q&A.

In the last chapter, when I said we had access to some of the leading experts in this business, I wasn't kidding.

David: *Is BlackBerry email encrypted as it is transmitted over the air to and from a BlackBerry device?*

Gary: Yes. Blackberry's wireless protocol includes encryption.

David: *Does all email traffic coming out of all BlackBerry devices travel over the RIM network? RIM is Research In Motion, the company that makes BlackBerry. This would seem to be the case from the big shutdown we saw in May of 2007.*

Gary: Yes. Email sent from BlackBerry devices is sent through the RIM network before connecting to the Internet.

David: *What is the topology and structure of the RIM network? Where do BlackBerry Enterprise servers, Lotus Domino servers, and Exchange servers figure in this topology?*

Gary: RIM's network topology is proprietary to RIM. BlackBerry Enterprise servers are software products companies buy. They are then installed on the company networks.

You don't need a BlackBerry Enterprise server to use email on a BlackBerry. Many carriers (T-Mobile, Verizon, etc.) allow email accounts on their networks to store email instead of an Enterprise server.

David: *How does BlackBerry traffic that comes from phone carriers and ISPs like AOL differ from other BlackBerry traffic? In other words, do we need to consider where Mr. Rove got his BlackBerry or do they all work the same?*

Gary: All BlackBerry devices work the same, but some offer more features than others. Email is transmitted via RIM's network. Additional features, like Web browsing, use different protocols (e.g., GPRS, General Packet Radio Service). Some functionality, like cell phone usage on a BlackBerry, uses the cell carriers network (Cingular, T-Mobile, etc.).

David: *Is there any known data logging that occurs on the BlackBerry network? Do RIM's servers or any other servers log emails sent through them? What are the constraints of those logs (how long, how big, how often)?*

In other words, is there any chance we'll find any of those allegedly missing email messages somewhere on a BlackBerry server?

Gary: No publicly-known accounting is done on the RIM network in terms of whose email went where. The emails that were stored on the email server for the RNC could be accessed via an email client on a computer or a BlackBerry. These are the ones that were "deleted by mistake."

David: *Can one BlackBerry send and receive from different email accounts? Is it more likely that Mr. Rove has one BlackBerry for his White House account and another for his RNC account or is he more likely to have a single device for both?*

How does the device get configured for choosing accounts to send and receive? And, if he does have one, does the traffic from both accounts run through the same servers and server infrastructure?

Gary: BlackBerry devices can be made to retrieve email from multiple accounts depending on the software in the BlackBerry and the configuration of the mail servers. How Karl Rove's email was configured and how it was routed is unknown.

[As we'll discuss in a later chapter, we subsequently found out, via Congressional testimony, that Mr. Rove used one BlackBerry for access to both official and RNC email. He's also lost his BlackBerry more than once.]

David: *What other questions should be answered about this and what other assumptions, conclusions, or technical observations can be made about White House staff use of BlackBerrys?*

Gary: Generally speaking, files don't get "deleted" without there being some form of retrieval. Weren't there any backups of their mail servers at all? There are many hard disk forensic tools that allow for the retrieval and analysis of "deleted files." I'm surprised that this process wasn't started immediately after discovering "emails were deleted."

What I learned from Gary

My discussion with Gary helped me understand more about BlackBerry usage, but left some doors open. For example, we now know it's possible that some email traffic to and from Mr. Rove's BlackBerry could have traveled through the Executive Office of the President servers and others, to and from the same BlackBerry, could have traveled through RNC servers located at SMARTech Corporation.

We know that over-the-air email transmission is encrypted, so at least messages going to and from the RIM network to Mr. Rove's BlackBerry (and those of other White House staffers) were reasonably secure. But that doesn't say much for where mail goes after it leaves the RIM network. And it doesn't say much about Mr. Rove's Outlook email client usage.

And it's this aspect of the whole discussion that worries me most.

An abundance of caution

On April 13, 2007, Deputy Press Secretary Dana Perino held a Press Briefing in addition to the "Gaggle" that we cited earlier. In that briefing, she implied that members of the White House staff, including Mr. Rove, used their *GWB43.com* Republican National Committee accounts to do official business:

> *MS. PERINO: I think that there were probably instances of that, but I think that was probably either out of an abundance of caution, or because of convenience. As I said, you're managing multiple email accounts, and plus we live in a world where we work 24/7. And I think that, again, there was no willful intention, but that there is a possibility that because you're using multiple accounts and trying to juggle that, that that was a problem. That's why we're working to fix it.*

> *Q Out of an abundance of caution they used their RNC accounts to do official business?*

> *MS. PERINO: Well, I think that when people have — I think there are gray areas — when they feel that there was a gray area that possibly they erred on the wrong side of it. I haven't seen copies of these emails, where they would — where these were described.*

From the perspective of abiding by the terms of the Hatch Act, this abundance of caution actually makes sense. In a similar situation, I might do the same thing.

Unfortunately, in an attempt to comply with the law, this abundance of caution may have created a considerable national security risk.

Tracing the path of a political email

Again, let me be clear I'm making all sorts of educated guesses here. I don't have detailed information to be sure this is what is actually happening. But what I'm about to discuss is, in general, how email works.

Let's first look at how email works when a message was sent from Mr. Rove's BlackBerry. It first traveled over an encrypted wireless connection from the BlackBerry to RIM's network. So far, so good.

But from RIM's network, it needs to travel to a destination server. This could be to somewhere on the RIM network, it could be to a Gmail account, or it could be to any other email server. The thing is, most email traveling *between* servers uses something called SMTP (Simple Mail Transport Protocol) and this email is completely unencrypted — wide open and easy for anyone to intercept.

So, an email message would have left his BlackBerry encrypted, but by the time it reaches the destination, it is likely to be completely open all along the rest of the way, free for anyone to intercept and read.

What about when Mr. Rove sent an email message from Outlook? Well, again, that can go a variety of ways, but let's assume he's used an Exchange server. Then, the message *might* travel to the Exchange server in an encrypted form. I said "might" because email messages traveling from Outlook to Exchange can be encrypted, but they can also be unencrypted. For now, though, let's give the White House IT geeks the benefit of the doubt and assume they set it up so his email goes from Outlook to Exchange in an encrypted form.

After that, the email again has to travel over the open Internet to the destination machine via completely unsecured SMTP.

What was once the President's confidential travel itinerary has just traveled all over the open Internet for anyone to intercept.

What about an incoming email? In this case, we know an incoming email message travels over unsecured SMTP to *GWB43.com,* which is a nice Postfix server. At this point, it likely gets forwarded to the RIM network or to an Exchange server, and, again, from SMARTech to Karl, it's probably secured.

The issue here is pretty simple. Once Mr. Rove's email (and that of all the other White House staffers) leave the home server, those messages are completely open to the world. They might be encrypted, but they can still be intercepted.

The nightmare scenario

Since Mr. Rove is no longer at the White House, let's use Joel Kaplan for our example this time. Kaplan is another Deputy Chief of Staff with responsibility for policy. Imagine that a staffer like Mr. Kaplan is sending an email to Deputy White House Press Secretary Dana Perino about the President's upcoming travel itinerary. Presidential security being what it is, it's fair to consider that itinerary confidential.

Let's look at how that message will travel in two scenarios: using the White House email system and using the RNC email system.

Using *EOP.gov,* everything should be safe. Both Dana Perino and the Deputy Chief of Staff have *EOP.gov* email accounts, which run internally to the Executive Office of the President. A message sent from Joel to Dana never travels over the open Internet and is going to be encrypted going from Mr. Kaplan's BlackBerry to Ms. Perino's laptop running Outlook. All is good.

But because of the Hatch Act, let's assume Mr. Kaplan is rightly practicing an abundance of caution. The President is about to make a speech in support of a member of Congress' reelection campaign. The email message to Ms. Perino is about the President's travel plans, exactly where he's going to go and what he's going to do while heading to the home district for our Congressman. This makes the message political, and, as such, by law can't run through *EOP.gov.*

Mr. Kaplan needs to send the message to Ms. Perino and he can't send it to her *EOP.gov* account. And he can't send it to her on *GWB43.com* because, as she mentioned in her March 27, 2007 Press Briefing, she doesn't have one:

> *Q How many people have those accounts?*
>
> *MS. PERINO: I think it's a handful, I don't think it's a lot. Obviously, the Office of Political Affairs, because they straddle these — both worlds. I know I don't have one.*

So where does that message go? It's going to go to a private email account Ms. Perino uses. It could be a Gmail account. It could be a Hotmail account. It could be an account from her own ISP. But for sure, it's not a secured account.

So the message leaves Mr. Kaplan's BlackBerry and travels via a secured wireless connection to RIM's servers. Then, this message with information about the President's confidential travel itinerary goes from a RIM server over the open Internet, quite possibly completely unencrypted, to Dana Perino's personal email account. Even if it was encrypted, encryption can be cracked.

What was once the President's confidential travel intinerary has just traveled all over the open Internet for anyone to intercept.

Of course, she decides to reply. As with many email messages, the original email message content is included, so the President's confidential travel itinerary now goes, via completely open and unencrypted SMTP, from Ms. Perino's ISP to the Postfix server run by SMARTech in Chattanooga. From there, it may be encrypted and forwarded to RIM, and from there to Mr. Kaplan's BlackBerry.

Anyone with $500 laptop and an Internet connection could easily intercept Mr. Kaplan's GWB43.com email to Dana Perino.

But the damage has already been done. What was once the President's confidential travel itinerary has just traveled all over the open Internet (twice!) for anyone to intercept. What if someone did? As we saw vividly in Chapter 1, this is the ultimate nightmare for the Presidential Protective Detail, charged with protecting the President from harm.

Our vastly superior technology isn't being used. Instead, *ad hoc* commercial systems run by "I know a guy in Chattanooga" are being used. Because of this, anyone with $500 laptop and an Internet connection could easily intercept Mr. Kaplan's *GWB43.com* email messages to Dana Perino. Any other email messages from the 1,000 politically-appointed White House staffers to any other political operatives could just as easily be intercepted.

There are so many variations to this scenario, including messages containing negotiation strategies, war management strategies, and any other form of official White House business that, instead of traveling over official, secured White House communications systems, are now completely open to the world.

Through an abundance of caution and a perfectly reasonable desire to abide by the law, the President's political staff could, unknowingly, be throwing caution to the wind — and possibly putting us all at risk.

Online resources

All of the links in this book are available from the book's Web site. Just visit *EmailsGone.com* and click on the Resources link. That way, you won't have to type in any long URLs.

Read the April 13 White House Press Gaggle at *http://www.whitehouse.gov/news/releases/2007/04/20070413-1.html*.

Read the Hatch Act at *http://www.osc.gov/ha_fed.htm*.

Visit Razorpoint Security at *http://www.razorpoint.com*.

Read the Presidential Records Act of 1978 at *http://www.archives.gov/about/laws/presidential-records.html*.

Read the Press Briefing at *http://www.whitehouse.gov/news/releases/2007/04/20070413-6.html*.

Read the March 27th Press Briefing at *http://www.whitehouse.gov/news/releases/2007/03/20070327-4.html*.

CHAPTER 8

An archiving plan only FEMA could love

As an editor, I'm always a little concerned when we run one of our in-depth special report series. I know many of our readers come to *OutlookPower*, *DominoPower* and the other ZATZ magazines for powerful tips and great reviews, while others love to dive into our deep analysis articles.

I am actually shuddering. And I'm a big dude. I don't normally shudder.

But when we run a special report series like the one on the controversy surrounding White House email, which eventually led to this book, some of our readers can't tear themselves away from the coverage, while others yearn for our more pedestrian fare. And, so, I'm always a bit worried that the decision to focus on one topic for a few months means we'll lose some of our readers who aren't necessarily interested in that topic.

When we dive into a subject like this, it's usually the case that no other publication anywhere is devoting the kind of depth to the issue that we are. There's the chance that we'll all get a deeper understanding of an important topic and we'll be able to share that understanding with others.

We've been told our willingness to take on important topics in incredible depth is one of the things that truly distinguishes us from other editorial teams and I have to agree.

When I published the first of the articles on this subject, I told the following to our readers. Dear Book Reader, I'll tell you as well:

- Keep reading. Keep learning.
- Tell your friends and colleagues about this work.
- Link to the book's Web site (it's at *http://www.EmailsGone.com*) on your sites and blogs.
- And, most important: talk about what you're reading to everyone you meet.

Let's all get a deeper, better understanding of what's going on. From there, perhaps we the people can help guide and influence decision makers to make the right decisions.

And now, let's get back to the topic at hand, the missing White House emails we've all been hearing about. Aren't these emails archived? How does the White House manage mail flow? Do they have an archiving system?

For that, we turn to the White House itself. In this chapter, we'll learn what White House spokesfolk Dana Perino and Tony Snow have been saying about the topic. After listening to them and reading the transcripts of press briefings in-depth, I've got with even more questions than we started with.

Of course, that's what makes this so darned interesting.

The West Wing meets the West Wing

Some of our magazine readers told me they were confused by the cast of characters and the positions they hold in our real life White House email docu-drama.

Figure 8-1. *From left to right, Tony Snow, Dana Perino, and Karl Rove.*

Let's see if I can clear that up for you by calling to mind the characters in a popular TV show and relating them to the real life White House staffers, shown in Figure 8-1, who I've been profiling in this book.

Real life Press Secretary Tony Snow does the same job as *The West Wing's* C.J. Cregg before she took over as Chief of Staff for Leo in the sixth season.

The surprisingly hot, real life Deputy Press Secretary Dana Perino does the same job as Annabeth Schott (I didn't know her last name either), played by Kristin Chenoweth in the television program.

The undeniably "or not hot" former Deputy Chief of Staff Karl Rove is an amalgam of Josh Lyman (before he went off and tried to run a comedy show), Sam Seaborn, and Toby Zieglar in his lucid years.

Of course, this brings us back to the President. George W. Bush is no Martin Sheen. Likewise, Martin Sheen is no Josiah Bartlet, even though he played him on TV. And to bring things full circle, Josiah Bartlet is no George W. Bush.

And, in a strange case of life riffing on art, Rudy Guliani is a freaky analog of Arnie Vinick, Barack Obama seems to be playing Jimmy Smits, and Hillary Clinton is doing her best to play Geena Davis in *Commander in Chief.* As a cautionary tale to Hillary, *Commander in Chief* lasted only barely into the first season, so read into that what you may.

Now that this is all as clear as mud, you'll get a good feel for what it's like to sift through the transcripts of White House Press Briefings. After days of reading and highlighting Tony Snow's and Dana Perino's comments, reading every single transcript from mid-March to mid-May 2007, I've started to feel like they're personally trying make me even crazier than I already am.

The mainstream media "reporters" who've been granted permission to sit in the White House Press Room are no help. They're asking questions like "That which you find when the forensics experts recover what it is that is lost, will you turn it over?" It makes you wonder if they've been blow-drying their hair just a few hours too long each day.

Seriously. That's a real quote.

Avoiding the political hatchet groups

As we continue our investigation, it's important to understand that there are a *lot* of sources I could pull information from. There are entire political organizations dedicated to digging up some dirt on the issue of these missing email messages, claiming scandal and worse. Many of those sources base their claims on reports and documents I've been unable to independently verify.

I actually spent an entire day reading *US v Libby Legal Proceedings* from the Office of Special Counsel Patrick J. Fitzgerald because one of those sources claimed a link between the proceedings and the missing email messages. I could find no such link and my day (and my patience) were both shot.

This is the crux of the problem for anyone attempting non-biased research.

Nearly all the fuss about the missing email messages comes from an entity with some political aim or another — immediately rendering those claims suspect. Since I'm *not* looking at this from a political angle, but really from a technical approach, I can't use any of those sources. It's crazy. Some of the sources these sites are claiming as "truth" are completely unverifiable.

One political organization (I'm not going to name it here) claims the source of its claims are from leaked documents within the White House. It might be true, but I can't verify it. And, it stinks of politics.

Reading the White House Press Briefings

I decided to pull my data straight from the White House press briefings. Before any of you go off on a rant about these being anything but unbiased, please understand I do know that.

Smoke 'em if ya got 'em.
You're going to need it.

Press briefings by any President's staff are designed to create specific impressions. However, it's reasonable to assume that anything positive claimed by a press briefing reflects the most positive possible marketing message while any mistake discussed in a press briefing reflects the mistake in the best possible light.

So, if the President's Press Secretary says email messages are "potentially lost," email messages are probably lost. What we can't be sure of is how many are lost, just how bad the situation is, and why they are lost. Given my skeptical nature, I've got to assume that if the President's office claims there are some messages missing, in reality, there are a *lot* of messages missing.

After all, one needs only to look at "I did not have sexual relations with that woman" and "Mission Accomplished" to see that Presidents tweak the truth to their own advantage.

The net of this is that by looking at the White House's own press briefings, we can get some anthropological indication of what we're dealing with, but certainly not the whole truth and nothing but the truth.

Missing White House emails

Deputy Press Secretary Dana Perino does confirm that some messages were "potentially lost" in her April 12, 2007 Press Briefing:

> *We are trying to understand to the best of our ability the universe of the emails that were potentially lost, and we are taking steps to make sure that we use the forensics that are available to retrieve any of those that are lost. And we've changed the policy so that we can make sure that this doesn't happen again.*

Perhaps Perino's comment here will shed some light on the question:

> *That is true at the White House for EOP accounts. I can't speak to any other organization, or their policies, although we are trying to work with the RNC to understand their policy.*

So far, the White House has acknowledged that some messages may be missing from government-run servers. But there's no specific detail on whether the political email has been archived, is missing, or what.

> **Question:** *What email messages are we talking about? Are we talking about email messages sent through the White House EOP.gov accounts or the messages sent through the RNC-operated GWB43.com accounts?*

But then we hit an interesting "whoops" in the road. According to Perino, apparently the RNC emails were deleted every 30 days up until 2004!

> *As I said, anyone with those emails here, as I understand it, since 2004, those emails have been separated from an RNC policy which is to automatically delete every 30 days deleted emails. So we have worked to try to be both in coordination and compliance with the Hatch Act, as well as the Presidential Records Act.*

There is no way this isn't going to be painful to wrap your head around. Further in Perino's briefing, she discusses an issue of "double-deleting." It's just easier if I let her tell you about it:

> *Q How does that square with what Scott Stanzel was saying this morning, where he was saying that staffers could, so-called, double-delete?*

> *MS. PERINO: That is true. When I say that we're trying to find if there were any potential emails that were not captured in that system, if someone had the capability to — if they wanted to clean out their inbox — delete a message, and then when your inbox — when your deleted box fills up, and you decide that you want to clean that up, if you delete that one, as well, where did those emails go? And that's exactly what we're trying to find out.*

> *Q A couple minutes ago you were saying that for sure since 2004 it's been archived, though. But I'm trying to understand, with the double-delete, can that override the archiving?*

MS. PERINO: I think that it might be able to. And I can't speak to any individual's personal email habits, but let me — I'm not a technical expert, so let me make sure we find that.

Q If it could override it, then what you said earlier about it's archived since 2004 may not be true, because it could be double-delete — some of the emails could be —

MS. PERINO: Let me look into the specific technical pieces of that.

Unfortunately, the White House briefing transcripts don't record who's asking the questions. But at least we're seeing Ms. Perino's answers. And, if I'm reading this correctly, she's saying email messages might be archived, and if they're archived, they could still be deleted later, if a user deletes mail from his or her Deleted Items folder.

Best practice archiving and the Deleted Items folder

Let's dive into this for a moment. If you're going to use best-practices to set up an email archiving solution, the solution would grab email messages as they transit the server.

Anything going in or out through the SMTP server would be archived to a central hard drive, which, every so often, should be backed up. There should be no way for a user on the network to delete or "double-delete" a message that exists on the archive server. In fact, there should be no way for a user to have any access whatsoever to the archive server.

We've run a number of articles on email archiving for regulatory compliance. In an article called "An interview with Roger Matus on email archiving and retrieval," reprinted in Appendix B, Roger helped us understand some of the issues involved in making sure your organization's email is archived and can be found in the event of a legal situation. Roger also helped us understand what your company can learn from the White House email problem, and wrote an article that's reprinted in Appendix C.

In an article called, "An interview with Marie Patterson on email storage and retrieval," reprinted in Appendix D, I had the opportunity to interview Marie Patterson, VP of AXS-One, a company that specializes in records management and compliance. While the topic of email storage and retrieval at first seems incredibly dry, once you read this interview, you'll be shocked at what could happen if you don't have good email storage and retrieval procedures in place.

What Ms. Perino's talking about is deleting messages in the user's own mail store, either in a local PST file or on an IMAP or Exchange Server. But even if a user deletes mail from the Deleted Items folder (the so-called "double-delete"), the archived email would still exist on the archive server. But, of course, that presupposes there *is* an archive server, which now seems a low probability.

> **Question:** *Is the White House operating a separate archive server or are they relying on each individual user to keep track of his or her email?*

Obviously, if there's no archive server, then we've got a serious IT management problem. But, honestly, that's almost impossible to believe. Almost.

Archiving political email

But what about archiving political email? Does the White House have a rock-solid IT policy for protecting political email from high-level White House staffers? Uh, not so much.

> *It is our understanding that since 2004 the RNC has excluded White House staff with RNC email accounts from their automatic 30-day deletion policy, though the RNC did not disable the user's capacity to*

manually delete emails until recent weeks. If users didn't manually delete messages from their computers since that time, the messages should be accessible. However, we cannot be sure that all communications dating from 2004 are preserved and that issue is part of the review process

Please understand that I'm writing this in a politics-neutral way. So when you read what I'm about to paste from the Press Briefing, understand that I couldn't make this up. There's just no way that any right-thinking IT person (or any email user of even marginal experience) could possibly come up with this approach.

Go ahead. Smoke 'em if ya got 'em. You're going to need it.

Q What is new?

MS. PERINO: Well, we have — it's clear, in regards to making sure people understand White House official business should be done on your White House official account. You should still endeavor to make sure that you don't have a Hatch Act violation. But one of the things that's new is that you have to — if you err on the side of using a political email, that you would also archive that some way.

So you would either print it off, or you would forward it to another email, to your personal account — I'm sorry, to your White House account, in some way keep that so that in the future, if the Counsel's Office needed to look back at those records, that they would have access to that. And in addition to that, I believe that individuals will just have to sign off that they got the policy and that they understand it, and that they will follow it.

Let's repeat this, just in case it didn't sink in. Just how is the White House going to archive political email? Here goes:

> *So you would either print it off, or you would forward it to another email, to your personal account — I'm sorry, to your White House account, in some way keep that so that in the future, if the Counsel's Office needed to look back at those records, that they would have access to that.*

You would either print it off or forward it to another email? Each of the 1,000 White House staffers with political roles — they're going to print or forward their messages, individually, with no management controls at all? Really?

I am actually shuddering. And I'm a big dude. I don't normally shudder. Yet, now, I am actually shuddering.

> **Question:** *Are they stoned?*

Seriously, this is the White House's solution for archiving political email? It can't be, can it? How could they have possibly come up with this plan? Don't they have qualified IT advisors?

> **Question:** *What, did they hire FEMA to come up with their email archiving program? Is Mike Brown the new IT czar at the White House?*

I can't possibly imagine that Jeff Averbeck, the guy operating the RNC servers down in Tennessee, would have signed off on this "plan." Seriously, White House people. If you don't want listen to me on this, go talk to Jeff. You've used him before, you know the guy, and from what I can tell of his systems and record, he seems to have something of a clue.

As always, there's more to the story, but after reading this transcript, I had to stop for now. This approach is *so* incomprehensibly badly thought out that either Ms. Perino's simply getting it wrong, or President Bush has to — immediately, without passing Go — shitcan whoever's coming up with his IT plans. *That's* one firing no one could possibly complain about.

I guess there is one other reason the White House could possibly be willing to run with an archiving plan so transparently unworkable. Maybe they actually *want* to lose some email messages.

Nah.

Online resources

All of the links in this book are available from the book's Web site. Just visit *EmailsGone.com* and click on the Resources link. That way, you won't have to type in any long URLs.

Read the US v Libby Legal Proceedings at *http://www.usdoj.gov/usao/iln/osc/index.html*.

Read the April 12, 2007 Press Briefing at *http://www.whitehouse.gov/news/releases/2007/04/20070412-5.html*.

CHAPTER 9

Migrating from Notes to Outlook

People, it seems, have some natural need to divide themselves up into tribes of various sorts. Religion, of course, is the most obvious. Some of us are Christians, some of us are Jews, some of us are Muslims.

Thousands in the U.K. and Australia consider themselves Jedi. Even a lack of belief becomes a religous affiliation of sorts, whether we're called Secular Humanists, Atheists, Free Thinkers, or something else.

Politics, of course, reflects the essence of tribalization. The division in America between Republicans and Democrats is obvious. Most people don't realize that both political parties have changed quite a bit since the early days.

In fact, Thomas Jefferson and James Madison founded the Democratic-Republican Party in 1792 (perhaps this explains why Bill Clinton and George Bush, Sr. can get along so well). At the time, the other party was the Federalist party — and, of course, those two parties even back then disagreed on economic and foreign policy issues.

This tribalization need within humanity has also reached into our choices of technology. There are devotees of the Macintosh who claim to hate the PC, and vice versa. There's the classic division between Linux lovers and Windows users. There are even "religious" differences between those coding Web sites in PERL, PHP, Ruby, and Java.

So is it any surprise at all that there's tribalization between those who use Lotus Notes and those who use Outlook, those IT people who install Microsoft's Exchange and those who install Lotus Domino?

As certain as it is that technology breaks, it's even more certain that users bitch.

Nope, there's no surprise here at all. This tribalization of enterprise collaboration systems makes particular sense when you factor in a reality about these two mail systems: it takes a long time to build towering expertise. If you've invested years in building your Lotus skills, you'll tend to gravitate to a Lotus solution. Likewise, if you've developed your expertise with Microsoft products, those are the solutions you'll want to install.

For us, here at ZATZ, it's become very interesting because we publish magazines for both tribes: *OutlookPower* is for the Microsoft messaging masses while *DominoPower* is for the Lotus-loving loquacious among us.

This perspective is going to become very important, because this transition between email systems is at the core of the White House's story about what happened to five million email messages.

For those of you who aren't techies, some of this chapter might be a challenge to read. Don't worry. Just skip over the techno-babble and read for the meat. There are some very serious concerns that came out of our analysis and this chapter delves into those concerns.

There are also some interesting claims from the White House that, if you don't know anything about Lotus Notes, might seem credible. However, if you *do* know something about how Notes works, you'll begin to realize that what the White House appears to be claiming just might not be true.

As always, the devil is in the details. It's time to look the devil in the eye.

What is Notes? What is Outlook?

Let's start by providing some background on these two technologies. Microsoft Outlook is an email program. It's used to compose and receive messages, organize lists of contacts, keep track of appointments, and track notes and memos. Lotus Notes does substantially the same thing, but is produced by IBM's Lotus Software group.

Notes and Outlook are part of the class of software called email clients. Email clients are programs that users like you and me see and interact with. Notes and Outlook also have server programs they connect to. Notes has a server program called Domino (and that's where the name *DominoPower* came from) while Outlook's server program is called Exchange.

Users rarely interact directly with the server, but that's the machine where much of the hard work is done. Here's an analogy. When you go into a nice restaurant, there's a waiter or waitress. You look at the menu and order a big, juicy prime rib. But in the back is a kitchen. The kitchen actually does all the preparation work, cutting the prime rib into slabs, seasoning it just so, and cooking it to perfection. The kitchen is the centralized machine.

Now, here's where the analogy breaks down, because computers and restaurants don't use the same language. In a restaurant, you're the client, the waitress is the server, and the kitchen is the kitchen. In the world of computers, you're the user, the waiter is the client program, and the kitchen is the server.

This stuff becomes very important when you realize that generally, Notes works with Domino and Outlook with Exchange. There are always exceptions (for instance, here at ZATZ, we use both Notes and Outlook, but our server programs are neither Domino nor Exchange). That's because, in general,

Domino and Exchange are meant for large organizations with hundreds of thousands of users and our mail server system here at ZATZ is scaled for our size company.

For home users, email is just email. You send and get messages and keep track of contacts. But for enterprise users like those in large corporations or at the White House, email is often more than just messaging and Notes and Outlook are more than just programs — they're application environments.

Now, what the heck does that mean? Simply, it means companies build upon the basic messaging functionality to add new features and capabilities. Knowledge management comes into play in these sorts of extended messaging applications, and groupware functions knit organizations together.

For example, a company might build a CRM (Customer Relationship Management) package on top of Outlook, so Sales can keep track of messages, who to call, and what happened in previous sales calls.

Another organization might build a purchase order tracking system on top of Notes, using Notes and Domino to control who requests and who approves a purchase order. For example, the tracking system might not let a low-level employee send a purchase order for approval straight to a company vice president. Instead, the routing function of the Notes-based application might require a supervisor's digital signature first.

Organizations live and die on their email systems. Most enterprise-level email systems consist not only of the email client programs like Notes and Outlook, but a batch of servers, backup systems, and custom applications. Moving from one email system to another is certainly possible, but it's not easy.

Both Microsoft and IBM have major efforts in place to convince enterprise customers to migrate from their competitor's environment to their own. Convincing an organization of size to switch is a big financial and PR win for the company who gets to install the new system. Microsoft and IBM have invested hugely in providing technologies and processes that make these migrations successful.

Given the efforts on the part of two of the biggest, most skilled, and most motivated technology companies to make migration doable, it's particularly curious to see what the White House's Dana Perino says might have caused all those email messages to have gone missing.

Migrating from Notes to Outlook

Interestingly, Dana Perino seems to confirm that email messages were lost, but she implies a different reasoning: a migration from Notes to Outlook that went bad.

Reading the April 13, 2007 Press Gaggle, Ms. Perino states:

> *Now, one of the things that occurred — and we're also trying to figure out how many emails possibly could be sent by 1,700 employees on a daily basis. I don't know if the numbers are staggering. My inbox is staggering so — we'll work to find that out. But there was a conversion sometime between 2002 and 2003 to convert people that were using Lotus Notes when we first arrived to Microsoft Outlook. And I know that the tech people worked to get us all transferred over. We had to save our Word documents and all to make sure that they weren't lost in that transition.*

In this, she's talking about moving from Notes to Outlook sometime in 2002 or 2003. She then states:

...that some of the emails would have been inadvertently lost in a transition of conversion of a technical sort.

She then ends this part of the discussion with the following exchange:

Q Dana, can I follow up on that real quick. So this allegation about the 5 million missing emails refers only, as you understand it, to this 2002-2003 time period?

MS. PERINO: I don't know the time period. I'm saying 2002-2003 because that's when I worked at CEQ, and that's when I know that I got — I moved from Lotus Notes to Microsoft Outlook. We'll get the dates for you. It was a rolling system in order to make sure that people weren't disrupted from their work.

CEQ is the Council on Economic Quality, part of the Executive Office of the President, where Ms. Perino was Communications Director.

So the real issue here is about migration. Could email messages have gotten lost in a migration from Lotus Notes to Microsoft Exchange?

Well, sure they could have. Never underestimate the ability for technology to go bad. And we should also never underestimate the ability for the government to hire the lowest bidder (except, I guess, for those no-bid contracts in Iraq, but that's not my editorial beat).

So it is certainly possible for the people who did the migration at the White House to have screwed up.

Yet, it shouldn't have happened. There are excellent tools for migrating from Notes to Outlook. After all, this is a *very* lucrative market opportunity for Microsoft.

Microsoft has a tool suite called the Application Analysis Envisioning Process (AAEP) for Lotus Notes application. Here's how Microsoft describes it:

> *The Application Analysis Envisioning Process (AAEP) for Lotus Notes applications provides a process to identify and classify Lotus Notes applications, understand their core components and functionality, and provide accurate guidance for recommended target solution. The primary goal of this process is to encourage a standard approach that can be used to define migration and target solution recommendations, as well as estimate migration costs and timelines.*

Microsoft also offers the Microsoft Transporter for Lotus Domino, which is described as:

> *Transporter Suite configures Directory and Free/Busy interoperability between Lotus Domino 6 or 7 and Exchange Server 2007 and Windows Server 2003 Active Directory and migration of users, mail and applications from Lotus Domino 5, 6 or 7 to Active Directory, Exchange Server 2007, and Windows SharePoint Services 3.0.*

The company also offers Microsoft Application Transporter 2006 for Lotus Domino, which even includes a Flash demo showing how the whole process is accomplished.

Further Microsoft resources for Notes and Domino migration can be found at their Resources for Interoperability and Migration from Lotus Domino page, which I list in the Online Resources section at the end of this chapter.

There are a number of other products that perform Notes to Outlook migration. These include Transend Migrator, XitNotes, Quest Notes Migrator for Exchange, OptimusBT, and quite a few others.

For Ms. Perino to imply that years of email messages were lost simply because a migration didn't go well vastly understates the scope of what had to go wrong for the migration to fail.

- There would have to have been a complete failure in backup strategy and execution.

- There would have to have been a complete failure in executing message migration.

The human factor

But there's one fundamental factor that neither of these conditional failure factors include: the human factor. By Perino's statement, there are 1,700 White House employees, presumably each with email.

Back in 2002 or 2003, when the email migration is said to have taken place, every single email user there would have had to *not notice* that they didn't get their old email messages when the migration was complete.

I don't know about you, but I live in my email. I am constantly looking back and referencing old email messages, some from yesterday, some from last week, and often some from last year. Think about this scenario:

- Email is migrated from Notes to Outlook, inconveniencing users and forcing them to get used to a new system.

- Each user logs into Outlook for the first time.

- Old messages from the previous system aren't there.

- Not a single user complains to the migration team.

- Those missing emails aren't discovered for four to five years.

It's just not plausible. Users bitch. As certain as it is that technology breaks, it's even more certain that users bitch. And when a migration goes bad, users are going to bitch even more. No one, anywhere, enjoys migrations and you're always going to have a cranky user population. Migrating email, which most people live in, is going to cause even more anxiety.

And you're telling me that in as hyper a place as the White House, migrating an email system in the middle of a war buildup, no one's going to complain when all their messages go missing?

Not likely. I just don't buy it.

Notes is designed to replicate messages

Now, here's another interesting factor. Lotus Notes is known for two key features, two key functions it does better than any other system on the market: replication and security. Every single Domino server and every single Notes client comes with some of the most sophisticated replication technology on the planet.

Notes databases are designed, out of the box, to duplicate themselves across servers and even from the server down to the individual user. It's as central to the DNA of the Lotus environment as photo ops are for politicians. In essence, Notes, by definition, is constantly backing itself up, over and over, across the entire network.

And that, again, leaves us with more questions than answers:

> **Question:** *Did the White House make regular backups?*

> **Question:** *What happened to those backups?*

> **Question:** *What happened to the Domino servers and their hard drives?*

> **Question:** *What happened to all the Notes replications?*

> **Question:** *How is it possible so many messages got lost and no one complained during the migration?*

Another possibility is that the email messages got lost and, as is the case in many companies when a network breaks, employees were told to just suck it up and move on. Theoretically, this could have happened back in 2002 or 2003 in the White House. But that brings us to another question.

> **Question:** *If a server blew up and all the past messages were lost, and everybody at the White House knew about it and had to deal with it, how come we haven't heard any "war stories" about the day the email died?*

Where have all the emails gone?

Migrating during wartime

On March 1, 2002, Operation Anaconda began and the U.S. invaded Afganistan. Also during 2002, a former FBI agent, Robert Hanssen was sentenced for selling secrets to Moscow, Jimmy Carter went to Cuba to visit with Fidel Castro, a car bomb exploded in Karachi, Pakistan in front of the U.S. Consolate, Worldcom and Enron were big economic news, the

Washington D.C. Beltway Sniper was on the prowl, and the mid-term elections for Congress took place.

Operation Iraqi Freedom, the Iraq invasion for Gulf War 2, took place on March 20, 2003. Prior to that time, the White House was actively involved in making preparations for the invasion, arguing over inspections, and otherwise making a fuss about alleged weapons of mass destruction.

On May 1, 2003, the "Mission Accomplished" speech took place on the aircraft carrier USS Abraham Lincoln (which, by the way, was outside San Diego, not anywhere near Iraq at the time). Subsequent to that speech, the White House was heavily involved in managing the post-invasion efforts in Iraq.

Also, during 2003, SARS (Severe Acute Respiratory Syndrome) was a big scare, killing 774 people before the World Health Organization declared it contained. On June 14, Robert Novak published the name of Valerie Plame, under cover for the CIA, and the whole CIA leak scandal began. On December 12, Saddam Hussein was captured in Tikrit and got a free dental exam. And, perhaps saddest of all, *Buffy the Vampire Slayer* aired its last show.

Before I close out this chapter, consider the following thoughts:

- Despite the cries of loyalists on the Microsoft side, Lotus Notes and Domino together make for an excellent email system, designed for security and reliability at the enterprise level.

- Email is absolutely essential for an organization like the White House to connect and collaborate.

- An email migration, even one that's as smooth as humanly possible, is going to cause communications interruptions for, at minimum, a few months.

To say that the White House was busy during 2002 and 2003 is, of course, a massive understatement.

> **Question:** *So, why, in the middle of a war, did the White House decide to change its email systems?*
>
> **Question:** *Isn't interrupting such a strategic communications system as email, in the middle of a war, the height of irresponsibility?*
>
> **Question:** *How could this have happened? Does the White House have any kind of formal policy in place that governs all aspects of email management? If so, what are the details?*
>
> **Question:** *Were strategic mistakes made because of unreliable email communications at the White House and in the Executive Office of the President before deciding to invade Iraq?*

No matter whether you're a Democrat or a Republican, you know that lack of communication breeds mistakes, misunderstandings, and crossed signals.

Email migrations don't happen by themselves. Someone had to authorize and decide to go forward with the migration, which, effectively, would have crippled email communication during that time.

So, here are the big, freaky questions of the day:

Question: *Could a crippled email system have led to strategic mistakes in Iraq?*

Question: *If doing this migration at this time wasn't irresponsibility, what was it?*

Question: *Could there have been any benefit to the administration for migrating right in the middle of the prewar buildup?*

Before some of you jump down my throat and say I'm writing this because I'm on one side or other, support one party or another, I swear I had no idea I'd come up with these questions before I started this investigation.

It's that last question that's had me thinking, especially as Congress is trying to get documents from the White House as part of their various investigations. If I were in the White House, is there any reason I would have wanted to cripple email at a critical time? Is there any reason I would want to be able to *say* email was crippled?

Maybe Senator Leahy was right. Maybe it's so they could claim the dog ate their homework. Maybe they wanted to create a foundation for later plausible deniability. Or maybe they just *really* don't understand email technology.

At least, those are some possibilities. I don't like the answers either way. I don't like the idea that it might have been a case of incredible irresponsibility. I also don't like the idea that this email failure was planned. But it's just not possible that losing those email messages was a simple accident. To be an accident, it would have needed an amazing array of rather impossible coincidences, especially given the intrinsic replication capabilities of Notes.

That's just the technical reality.

Online resources

All of the links in this book are available from the book's Web site. Just visit *EmailsGone.com* and click on the Resources link. That way, you won't have to type in any long URLs.

Read the April 13, 2007 Press Gaggle at *http://www.whitehouse.gov/news/ releases/2007/04/20070413-1.html.*

Learn more about Microsoft's Application Analysis Envisioning Process (AAEP) at *http://www.microsoft.com/downloads/details. aspx?familyid=AE068FF4-75C0-4DDB-B632-AC639762D9F4&displaylang=en.*

Learn more about Microsoft Transporter for Lotus Domino at *http://www. microsoft.com/downloads/details.aspx?FamilyId=35FC4205-792B-4306-8E4B-0DE9CCE72172&displaylang=en.*

Learn more about Microsoft Application Transporter 2006 for Lotus Domino at *http://www.microsoft.com/downloads/details.aspx?FamilyId=CF4EFD6E-ECDD-435F-926E-4C9B828526F1&displaylang=en.*

Learn more about Microsoft's Resources for Interoperability and Migration from Lotus Domino at *http://technet.microsoft.com/en-us/interopmigration/ bb403105.aspx.*

Learn more about Transend Migrator at *http://transend.com.*

Learn more about XitNotes at *http://www.lotus-notes-export.com/XitNotes. asp?s=gUS-LotusNotesExchange.*

Learn more about Quest Notes Migrator for Exchange at *http://www.quest. com/notes-migrator-for-exchange/*.

Learn more about OptimusBT at *http://www.optimusbt.com/migrations_ consulting.htm?gclid=CJmc_ZXOrIwCFQ5HVAodkT1aRQ*.

Tips from the ZATZ magazines

Migrating isn't just about moving email messages, although that's a big portion of the job.

Moving from one system to another involves moving all the contents of all the email system databases, including messages, contacts, scheduling information, histories, and more. It also involves rebuilding, duplicating, or re-engineering the custom applications (like CRM or purchase order management) built on top of the message solution.

It also means making sure every user has new software and is trained to use it.

CHAPTER 10

Why did Karl Rove keep losing his BlackBerry?

Karl Rove, former Senior Advisor to the President of the United States, has been one of the most powerful people in Washington. He conducted a vast amount of political and official business via his BlackBerry. He also apparently regularly lost his BlackBerry.

Somewhere out there are a couple of BlackBerry devices with a potential mother lode of confidential or even classified information.

You would think that when someone this central to the management of the United States government loses something, loses something so integral to high-level communication, and apparently loses it *repeatedly* — well, you'd think someone would care. In fact, you'd think that the House committee investigating Karl Rove's email usage would pick up on this detail during testimony that took place in front of its own committee members.

Nope. No such luck. Look up the phrase "Can't see the forest for the trees" and you'll see our illustrious Congress. Can you say "National Security Risk?" Sure. I knew you could.

And, not only did the House Committee on Oversight and Government Reform overlook this little detail — even when the testimony took place right in front of them — so did all of mainstream media. Whether you watch CNN or Fox News, read the *New York Times*, or even *Time Magazine,* none of these media giants picked up on the fact that somewhere out there are a couple of BlackBerry devices with a potential mother lode of confidential or even classified information.

So why do I have this scoop when everyone else missed it? I actually do my homework.

Rather than reading and reprinting the same press release everyone else did, I actually read through *all* of the testimony, making notes, and tracking down what's really going on. Ain't nothin' more boring than congressional testimony, but if you let the boring get to you, you might miss the meat.

We'll get back to Mr. Rove and his missing BlackBerry devices in a few minutes. For now, let's look at what Congress did actually pay attention to. It's a little boring, but it's worth reading for the meat.

Possible Presidential Records Act violations

Working on an in-depth project like this analysis of the White House email controversy can be something of a moving target. While we're working here at ZATZ to understand all the intricacies of the inner-workings of White House email, the United States Congress is also hard at work, trying to find some sort of smoking gun to further their political aims.

In June 2007, the House Committee on Oversight and Government Reform of the 110th Congress released a report entitled *Interim Report: Investigation of Possible Presidential Records Act Violations,* which came to some disturbing conclusions about the White House's use of email — and lack of preservation of the message traffic involved.

Let's revisit why keeping presidential records is important. Sure, there's historical value. It's nice for future generations of historians to be able to go back and learn about the inner workings of a given administration in its own voice. It's also nice for future administrations to look back and understand the reasoning behind certain decisions and actions, to help with future decisions and actions.

Of course, the real juicy-juice in the Presidential Records Act is for the benefit of an opposing Congress, like the one we have now. Email is a very free-form and casual form of communication. You and I say things in email we'd rather not preserve for posterity. The same is true of Presidential officials and their use of email. Our favorite Congress-critters figure that if they dig through enough Presidential email, they'll find something nasty they can use to beat over the heads of their rivals.

White House record-keeping, as it pertains to email, is for crap.

So, even though it's the law that Presidential administrations keep track of email messages sent and received, you can imagine complying is not something administrations do with excessive enthusiasm. And given that the Bush Administration has been more closed to outside scrutiny than most modern administrations, you can imagine that President Bush's team hasn't gone out of their way to make email archiving a top priority.

Therefore, it's no real surprise that the general conclusions of the report indicate a substantial lack of email archiving:

- Rather than a "handful" of RNC-related email accounts that Deputy Press Secretary Dana Perino originally stated existed, or even the 50 that Perino later reported, there were 88 RNC-based political email accounts operating at the White House.

- Of the 88 White House officials who received RNC email accounts, the RNC has preserved no email messages for 51 officials.

- The RNC has preserved 140,216 messages sent or received by Karl Rove. Over half of this email (75,374 messages) was sent to or received from individuals using official *.gov* email accounts.

- The RNC has preserved only 130 pieces of email sent to Mr. Rove during President Bush's first term and no email sent by Mr. Rove prior to November 2003. For many other White House officials, the RNC has no email records from before the fall of 2006.

- In addition, there are major gaps in the email records of the 37 White House officials whose email the RNC did preserve.

- Finally, apparently, there is evidence that the Office of White House Counsel under Alberto Gonzales may have known that White House officials were using RNC email accounts for official business, but took no action to preserve these as Presidential records.

As has been the case thus far in this special analysis, rather than gather information second-hand from mainstream press reports, we're going directly to the source. In the next few pages, I'll show you my analysis of the report itself and some fascinating facts found by careful reading of congressional testimony.

The House report

Unfortunately, the House report only explores one aspect of the email crisis I've uncovered at the White House: poor archiving. As I mentioned earlier, politicians are more interested in finding some juicy tidbit within Presidential records than they are with broader technical implications.

...yet another thing overlooked by the Oversight Committee.

My analysis has found that the record-keeping issues related to White House email are of the least concern when it comes to national security. Of far more concern are other aspects of White House email that the Oversight committee completely overlooked. It's these aspects I've discovered in my own investigation. For now, though, let's continue with what did not escape the sight of the Oversight committee.

In this case, it's the Democrats chasing after the Republicans, but in prior years, Republicans have certainly done their fair share of politically motivated investigating. Even though this House committee's motivations can't be considered pure, there's no doubt their conclusions mirror some of our observations. Put bluntly, White House record-keeping, as it pertains to email, is for crap.

One interesting aspect of the Committee's report is the use of the word "destroyed," as in this sentence from the report:

> *At this point in the investigation, it is not possible to determine precisely how many presidential records may have been destroyed by the RNC.*

From a technical perspective, I doubt the email messages in question were actually destroyed. I think they were simply not preserved. This seems a subtle difference, but it is major and it reflects the key difference between paper and digital records.

If there was a paper memo and it was eliminated in some way, a conscious action on the part of an individual would have had to take place to destroy the paper document, whether by shredding, burning, dumping in the trash, or giving it to the dog to eat.

Here's what the report had to say:

> *Whether intentionally or inadvertently, it appears that the RNC has destroyed a large volume of the emails of White House officials who used RNC email accounts. The RNC has told the Committee that it had a "document retention" policy under which emails that are more than 30 days old are deleted. In addition, the RNC has said that individual account holders had the ability to delete permanently emails less than 30 days old. As a result of these policies, potentially hundreds of thousands of White House emails have been destroyed, many of which may be presidential records.*

When a message is transmitted by email, it's an ephemeral thing, existing only in flipped bits that pass from client to server to client. Sure, the message could be stored at any point along the way, but the default design behavior of most email servers is to generally avoid preservation, simply in order to keep the disk storage load low. If a message doesn't exist any more, it's not necessarily because someone took a specific action to destroy it. Rather, it's likely that someone did *not* take a specific action to preserve it.

In an earlier article, I talked about the security risk inherent in having someone like Mr. Rove send email correspondence via an outside service, like that run by SMARTech, a small Chattanooga ISP. The following statement from the Committee's report gives us some additional quantification:

> *Mr. Rove and six other White House officials — Mike Britt, Jonathan Felts, Korinne Kubenna, Mindy McLaughlin, Cliff Rosenberger, and Nick Sinatra — all averaged more than 100 emails sent or received each weekday that their accounts were active. In 2007, Mr. Rove frequently sent more than 100 emails per day through his RNC email account and received more than 200 per day.*

Calculating out Mr. Rove's use across six years, it looks like he received about 438,000 messages and sent about 219,000 messages. As I discussed back in Chapter 7 "The nightmare scenario," these were all sent via the general Internet and were likely all completely open for anyone to intercept.

You can begin to see more of the security risk involved when you look at how apparently unsecured RNC accounts were used to send mail to more secure *.gov* accounts. Here's what the report had to say:

> *The Committee asked the RNC to provide data on how many emails each White House official sent to or received from official ".gov" email accounts. According to the information from the RNC, virtually all of the 37 White House officials used their RNC accounts to communicate with government officials with official ".gov" email accounts. Of the 674,367 emails preserved by the RNC, 240,922 emails (36%) were sent to or received from government email accounts. Four White House officials — Karl Rove, Jason Huntsberry, Melissa Danforth, and Emily Willeford — conducted more than half of their communications on their RNC accounts with government officials who were using official ".gov" accounts. Mr. Rove alone sent or received 75,374 ".gov" emails using his RNC email account.*

Introducing Susan Ralston

The Oversight Committee took the deposition of Susan Ralston, Mr. Rove's former executive assistant, on May 10, 2007. Ms. Ralston was the star witness in this investigation and is cited 35 times in the 16-page report. Prior to working for Mr. Rove, Ms. Ralston was the Assistant Director of Governmental Affairs at Greenberg Traurig.

Her testimony was key to the Oversight Committee's report. And it was in the pages of this testimony that I discovered Mr. Rove's proclivity for losing BlackBerry devices.

Key observations from Ms. Ralston's testimony

Let's get to the most interesting observation first. On Page 19, Line 10 of her testimony was this seemingly innocuous paragraph:

> *It may have been four or five times. I can't say specifically, but it seemed to be a number of times. Karl would get a new computer. He would lose a BlackBerry. Whenever this happened, there would be some conversation with the IS&T people about his mail file.*

That's it. That's the only mention of the subject. Just, as a matter of course, *"He would lose a BlackBerry."* Why the investigators asked no further questions on this topic is just a mystery.

We all know what a BlackBerry can hold. It can hold a lot of email correspondence. It can hold phone numbers, contact information, calendar information, and even documents. And Mr. Rove, then Deputy White House Chief of Staff, with access to the White House Situation Room, the sanctum sanctorum of American security and strategy, would lose his BlackBerry.

Question: *How many BlackBerry devices did Mr. Rove lose?*

Question: *What sort of information was on each BlackBerry when it was lost?*

Question: *What efforts were taken to recover these missing devices and their potentially classified information?*

I also got some other useful insights from Ms. Ralston's testimony. For example, I now know that Mr. Rove had three email accounts, a political email account, a White House email account, and a personal email account running on AOL.

Other details from the testimony that relate to our discussion include:

- During the Plame leak investigation, Patrick Fitzgerald and his team took Mr Rove's political laptop and his BlackBerry. This would mean that some of his records are likely in the hands of the Special Prosecutor.

- Apparently, during the leak investigation, Ms. Ralston testified that she and Mr. Rove were instructed to "go and do keyword searches, based on the subpoena that we got, and search all of his folders for keywords." While I agree that government oversight is a good thing, this activity seems like a poor use of time. First, the investigators asked the investigatees to find self-incriminating evidence — yeah, that'll really happen! Second, the time of a key government official was spent sifting through keyword searches.

- Rove printed many of his email messages. Specifically, "Well, if there was follow-up action or it was something lengthy that he would 1ike to read later, he would print it out. He would often get a lot of articles to read, so they would be things to print out and then look at later."

- These printouts were managed by a government entity called "Records Management," which was responsible for all the files storage in Mr. Rove's office.

- Mr. Rove only had one BlackBerry (at a time, apparently). He did, however, have two phones.

I also discovered that Mr. Rove has a domain name, *ROVE.com*. A quick Whois shows that *ROVE.com* is managed by PrismNet.com, a Texas ISP, as shown in Figure 10-1.

He's had that domain since 1995, about halfway through George W. Bush's first term as Governor of Texas. This gets somewhat interesting because of the following testimony by Ms. Ralston:

> *Well, it was — it wasn't — I don't know how you would classify it, but it was a "Rove.com" email address. There were, I can't remember when, but at some point his Rove.com emails all went to the same political account. So if you sent an account, if*

Figure 10-1. *Karl Rove has had the ROVE.com domain name since 1995.*

*you sent an email to George W. Bush.com or if you sent an email to him
at Rove.com, it went to the same place.*

My analysis shows that *ROVE.com's* MX records actually point to
PrismNet.com's own mail server, a Sendmail server, as shown in Figure 10-2.

While I can't tell for sure whether email to *ROVE.com* routes indirectly to
GWB43.com, if it does, it's not set up at the DNS level. So, at least in this,
Ms. Ralston's testimony may be mistaken.

> **Question:** *If Ms. Ralston is mistaken about Mr. Rove's ROVE.com
> account, could she also be mistaken about other aspects of her testimony?*

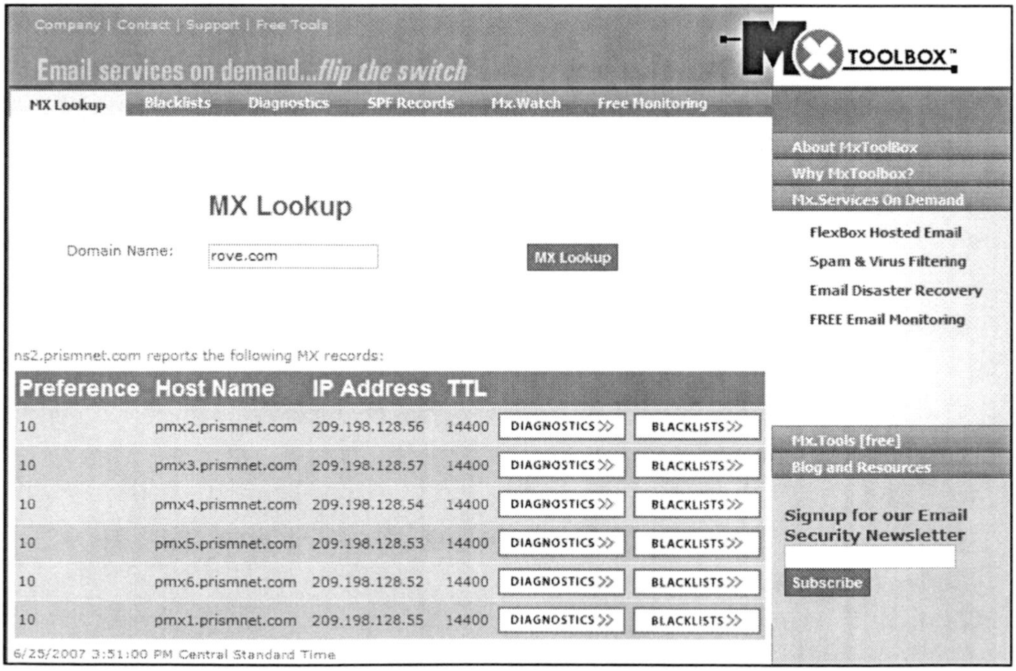

Figure 10-2. *It doesn't look like ROVE.com email is being forwarded anywhere.*

Conclusions

What have we learned from all this? My biggest concern is, once again, national security. I don't know how many of Mr. Rove's BlackBerry handhelds are floating around out there, but losing even one could be dangerous.

This is a bigger issue than Mr. Rove, of course, especially since he's no longer at the White House in the Deputy Chief of Staff role. The big issue here is, once again, one of security. Those little devices hold a lot of information, many White House staffers use them, and probably quite a few lose them.

The Committee's results reinforced what we already knew: archiving for RNC-based email records is quite inconsistent. We also know that the White House's plan for future archiving is also inconsistent, yet another thing overlooked by the Oversight Committee.

Before this report was issued, along with Ms. Ralston's testimony, I thought I'd discovered all of the problem areas related to email in the White House. I found myself quite disturbed to see there's yet another big problem area: losing BlackBerry handhelds. This problem, too, needs a comprehensive management strategy so it doesn't continue.

Question: *Is Mr. Rove the only one who misplaces these things?*

Question: *Are other key White House staffers losing their communications devices?*

Question: *Just how many times is someone allowed to lose a BlackBerry before being told, "No more"?*

Online resources

All of the links in this book are available from the book's Web site. Just visit *EmailsGone.com* and click on the Resources link. That way, you won't have to type in any long URLs.

Read the Interim Report: Investigation of Possible Presidential Records Act Violations at *http://oversight.house.gov/documents/20070618105243.pdf*.

Read Susan Ralston's testimony at *http://oversight.house.gov/documents/20070618105351.pdf*.

Visit PrismNet.com at *http://www.prismnet.com*.

Tips from the ZATZ magazines

Think just because your BlackBerry is encrypted or password protected, it's safe? Think again.

Two scary news items from *DominoPower Magazine* reinforce our message about the need for improved security. In "Hijacked handheld turns data spy," at *http://www.dominopower.com/newsitems/00022297.html*, a Blackberry can be "blackjacked," turning the popular mobile email device into a backdoor into corporate networks.

In "Elcomsoft password recovery," at *http://www.dominopower.com/newsitems/00025368.html*, our news editor shows how a simple program can "recover" passwords from most locked file formats.

CHAPTER 11

Understanding the root causes

Ever since electronic mail has been used at the White House, there's been controversy over how electronic mail is used at the White House. For White House staffers, email is an intrinsic and necessary communications tool, greasing the gears that make the White House run smoothly. For members of Congress, usually members of the opposing party, email at the White House is a potential treasure trove of incriminating evidence, a nearly guaranteed smoking gun.

Is IT management at the White House as incomprehensibly unprofessional as it seems — or is a pretense of cluelessness being used to divert questions of disclosure?

I started this investigation asking pretty much the same question Senator Patrick Leahy and Representative Henry Waxman asked, *"Where have all the emails gone?"* They were, of course, referring to email messages that might incriminate the Bush II administration in the Democrats' investigation into the firing of eight United States Attorneys.

However, after five months of very in-depth research, I've come to the conclusion that the missing email messages are the least of our concerns. After completion of my in-depth analysis, I determined that White House email use can be summed up with five key concerns:

- Email has always been an issue with Presidents since email existed.

- The Hatch Act is encouraging poor email security, routing mail through the open Internet, and creating potential national security risks.

- There is no acceptable archiving methodology in use.

- A seemingly unnecessary email system migration occurred at the worst possible time.

- There appears to be poor management of portable technology (people are losing their toys).

Email priorities

Despite Congress' desire to have something with which to beat up the White House, when it comes to email use in the White House, I recommend that operational priorities should be in this order:

- National security is more important than archiving.

- Archiving is more important than disclosure.

- Disclosure is important for an informed populace.

- An informed populace can sometimes be counter to national security.

Let's look at each of these in turn.

National security is more important than archiving

As you've seen in my worst-case scenarios, some really bad things can happen as a result of poor email security and continuity.

Even though the intent is that taxpayer money not fund political activity — and that incumbents don't have the benefit of government services in running their campaigns — it's very clear that even the most benign-seeming email message, falling into enemy hands, could cause severe damage.

Archiving is more important than disclosure

No administration (in fact, no organization, and virtually no individual) can withstand an exhaustive examination of every email message ever sent. Could you? I certainly couldn't. Email is a form of casual communication and when people communicate casually, they often say the types of things you would say when you're communicating casually.

Has the Hatch Act been used as an excuse to bypass government servers, thereby giving a reasonable-sounding excuse to circumvent the Presidential Records Act and the Federal Records Act?

Any large body of email messages is going to have some incriminating material in it. In a climate where there's such partisanship at such high levels in America's government, the safest path for most administrations must simply seem to be "losing" all that email — or at least creating conditions where losing the bulk of the messages is easy and wrongdoing is plausibly deniable.

And yet, they need to keep track of this stuff. There can be no excuse for losing large amounts of email messages. Even if the message archives are never used for any oversight purpose, they're an important part of the historical record and there may come a day when a particular message or message trail is critically needed.

Disclosure is important for an informed populace

In a world where Paris Hilton's jail sentence and Britney's shaved head is more important (and more tangible) to most Americans than items of policy, the value of an informed populace may seem to come into question.

After all, more people watch NASCAR than read *The New York Times.* Courtesy of partisan politics and an excellent disinformation distribution channel, a surprisingly large group of people now side with Anne Coulter's contention that her "only regret was that Timothy McVeigh didn't hit the *New York Times* building."

The question is obvious, "Can our populace be informed, and can they tell truth from crap?" More and more people today get their information from late night comedy like the left-leaning *Daily Show with Jon Stewart,* right-wing agitators like Ms. Coulter, and conservatively-biased news channels like *Fox News.* After all, to many citizens, why get your news from an impartial source when you can listen to people you generally agree with?

And yet, disclosure is important. While nearly half of all Americans will always vote Democrat and nearly half of all Americans will always vote Republican, there remain a core group of citizens who want to know what's really going on. These people deserve to be informed.

Further, in a world where it's possible to replace a voting machine's internal programming circuitry in less than a minute — there's a video circulating on YouTube demonstrating this — our citizenry may be our last, best hope for the preservation of a truly democratic republic.

An informed populace can sometimes be counter to national security

Yet, sometimes information shouldn't be set free. Let's look at an example from the tech world. Bugs and exploits are regularly discovered in computer operating systems like Microsoft Windows. Sometimes, they're discovered by evildoers and those exploits eventually wind up hurting us all. But sometimes those bugs and exploits are discovered by computer security professionals.

It's a matter of generally accepted practice that when a security professional discovers an exploit in, say, Internet Explorer, the exploit is reported to Microsoft first, giving them a chance to fix the bug. In this way, information about the exploit isn't made public before a patch can be created in the software and users' systems updated with the fixed defensive measure.

Unfortunately, there have been times when tech companies have disregarded critical bug reports from security professionals. In these cases, security professionals have released information to the public as a way to force the bugs to be fixed. Obviously, it's a risk, because then an "arms race" may ensue. Will the bad guys release an exploit into the wild before the software can be patched to defend against it?

I've debated a similar issue in first writing the article series and then this book. I've exposed some serious vulnerabilities in how the White House manages email. Unfortunately, based on analysis I did over time, reading over press briefings, Congressional testimony, tracing email flow, and looking at the history of email use at the White House, it became clear just how unlikely it is that any administration will fix their email problems without outside pressure.

Given that we here at ZATZ reach more email professionals than any other publisher, it seemed prudent to publish the article series and inform the experts. With an informed expert populace, some of whom work on IT systems for the government, it seemed far more likely that improvements could be made to a clearly broken system by the very experts who would be called on to do the job..

There's always a balance between too much disclosure and necessary disclosure. The U.S. House Permanent Select Committee on Intelligence performs oversight of the American intelligence community. Much of what they discuss must, of necessity, remain behind closed doors. In this case, there's oversight, but also security. And that's how it should be.

Likewise, while it's important that all White House email be archived, and it's important that some of that email be available for disclosure, some may always need to remain secret.

Root causes

After detailed examination, I've identified three root causes for the identified problems with White House email: the nature of politics, the Hatch Act of 1939, and no coherent, administration-spanning IT operations directorate.

The nature of politics

Ain't nothin' going to fix the nature of politics, but the other two stand a chance of correction. In fact, it's my conclusion that both the Hatch Act and a lack of a professional IT agency feed off each other, creating the situation we Americans now find ourselves in.

The Hatch Act of 1939

The Hatch Act is a strange beast. It was originally created as a way to prevent Federal employees from joining any organization whose goals included the overthrow of the United States government.

Today, the Hatch Act allows Federal employees to participate in political parties, but prohibits them from engaging in political activity while on duty.

The goal behind the use of the Hatch Act was quite honorable, and its goal of preventing Federal funds from being used for political purposes is laudable.

Unfortunately, it has had two unintended side effects with regard to White House email:

- It forces White House staffers to use private-sector resources for communication, bypassing all of the government's security resources.

- It gives politicians in the White House an excuse for bypassing Presidential Records Act requirements.

  Question: *Has the Hatch Act been used as an excuse to bypass government servers, thereby giving a reasonable-sounding excuse to circumvent the Presidential Records Act and the Federal Records Act?*

Amateur-hour IT

Email management in the White House seems shoddy, at best. It is beyond comprehension that an archiving policy stated in a Presidential press briefing should consist of "printing it out" or forwarding email messages to another account.

In my professional opinion, it was completely irresponsible for the White House to change email systems during the build-up to war.

And, of course, the idea that many White House staffers are sending potentially unsecured email messages via some podunk ISP in the middle of Tennessee — well, that would be funny if it weren't so sad and true.

This form of unsupervised information technology management, with IT teams that change as administrations change, and with procedures that are clearly *ad hoc* at best — this is at the root of why excuses like "we lost the messages during migration from Notes to Outlook" seem plausible to outsiders.

> **Question:** *Is IT management at the White House as incomprehensibly unprofessional as it seems — or is a pretense of cluelessness being used to divert questions of disclosure?*

In the next chapter, I'll dive right into my recommendations. There are six key actions that need to be taken. If taken soon, with appropriate care and oversight, these actions should resolve the problems I've shown you and prevent some of the disastrous scenarios I've explored.

Online resources

All of the links in this book are available from the book's Web site. Just visit *EmailsGone.com* and click on the Resources link. That way, you won't have to type in any long URLs.

Watch the YouTube video demonstrating a 60-second voting machine hack at *http://www.youtube.com/watch?v=EowKalRT3lc.*

Since YouTube videos have a tendency to disappear, you can also find voting machine hacks by simply typing "voting machine hack" into the YouTube search field.

CHAPTER 12

My formal recommendations

If you take anything at all away from this book, let it be this: email in the White House needs to be fixed. Based on my analysis, I've come up with six specific recommendations:

- The Hatch Act is in conflict with national security concerns with regard to White House email and must be amended to allow, if not require, White House staffers to use secured government systems for all email communication — political or otherwise.

- White House email needs to be managed by a dedicated IT team that lives across administrations, with a professionalism and procedural base similar to the Secret Service Presidential Protective Detail.

- Political email for incumbents also needs to be managed by the same team.

- Archiving needs to be managed by this same IT team, and the entire cumulative library of archives will need to be checked and migrated every four years as technology and file formats change.

- We need a better understanding of phone/BlackBerry use, especially if these things get lost. I recommend that all mobile phones used by White House staffers be managed by this same IT team.

- Although not directly an email issue, the conflict between the intent of the Presidential Records Act and Executive Order 12,233 needs to be explored. Information must be made free.

Let's discuss each in turn.

Recommendation: change the Hatch Act and/or its official guidelines

The U.S. Office of Special Counsel lists a series of guidelines for executive branch employees of the federal government. These guidelines are:

These federal employees may:

- *Be candidates for public office in nonpartisan elections*
- *Register and vote as they choose*
- *Assist in voter registration drives*
- *Express opinions about candidates and issues*
- *Contribute money to political organizations*
- *Attend political fundraising functions*
- *Attend and be active at political rallies and meetings*
- *Join and be an active member of a political party or club*
- *Sign nominating petitions*
- *Campaign for or against referendum questions, constitutional amendments, municipal ordinances*
- *Campaign for or against candidates in partisan elections*
- *Make campaign speeches for candidates in partisan elections*
- *Distribute campaign literature in partisan elections*
- *Hold office in political clubs or parties*

These federal employees may not:

- *Use official authority or influence to interfere with an election*
- *Solicit or discourage political activity of anyone with business before their agency*
- *Solicit or receive political contributions (may be done in certain limited situations by federal labor or other employee organizations)*
- *Be candidates for public office in partisan elections*
- *Engage in political activity while on duty, in a government office, wearing an official uniform, using a government vehicle, and*
- *Wear partisan political buttons on duty*

It's quite obvious that the Hatch Act is bent just a little bit for the President of the United States. For example, clearly political activity (even if just a discussion among staffers) occurs on Air Force One, which is very much a government vehicle.

The Hatch Act must not be used as an excuse or as a guideline for running political email outside the government's security apparatus.

What I find interesting and curious is that the neither the Hatch Act itself nor the government's posted guidelines have been amended to explicitly discuss the use of email and whether or not it can be run through government servers.

In the previous chapter, I asked the question, "Has the Hatch Act been used as an excuse to bypass government servers, thereby giving a reasonable-sounding excuse to circumvent the Presidential Records Act and the Federal Records Act?"

It's an interesting question, and while it does pertain to the disclosure concerns I've identified, it does not pertain to the national security concerns.

Put simply, the Hatch Act must not be used as an excuse or as a guideline for running political email outside the government's security apparatus.

It'd be as if the President had to fly commercial if he was going to give a speech supporting someone's campaign. The idea is ludicrous. Whether we like it or not, the President makes a juicy target for our enemies. America has learned that, and we've put a series of very well-trained teams in charge of the President's protection and all aspects of the President's transportation.

Unfortunately, whether politicians like it or not, email routed outside of secured channels also makes a juicy target for America's enemies. Every email sent by a White House staffer via the open Internet, via SMARTech, or even via AOL is a target. Even if the staffer is a 30-year-old deputy-level White House employee confirming a date via AOL, the message is a target — and so is the staffer, and so is his date.

I wish I could say I'm just being paranoid, but the world is full of troubling people and there are countries, organizations, and entities that wish to see us compromised.

Whether it's an *al-Qa'idah fatwa*, anti-Americanism from Turkey's *Adalet ve Kalkinma Partisi*, troubles with Iran's Mahmoud Ahmadinejad, rhetoric from Venezuela's Hugo Chavez (who virtually foams at the mouth when speaking of President Bush as a "devil", a *pendejo,* and "Mister Danger"), or the more serious threat that seems to be wafting out of an ever more militant Russian Federation, there are governments and enemy entities that could derive some advantage from the primo intelligence that could be gathered from intercepting White House email messages.

I recommend that the Hatch Act guidelines be officially amended to state that all email and other electronic communication from senior White House personnel be subject to management through secure government systems.

It should be clear that whether a staffer is lower level or more senior is not nearly as relevant as access to information, no matter how innocuous that information might seem. Anyone whose communications could possibly cause a risk should be required to use secure government systems. Period.

Further, this should encompass all email communication by such staffers, including personal communication. Whether it's a note about going on a date or a note about picking up milk, those email messages (and, by extension, instant messages as well) should be managed by secure government oversight.

I fully understand that such a requirement may seem draconian, but this is not a game. A simple "The President is away, so I don't have to work late" message could provide all sorts of insights into scheduling that America might not want its enemies to have.

Recommendation: establish an Electronic Communication Protection Detail

Imagine if each President had to hire "some guy" to protect him while out in public. That was the case for all Presidents before Teddy Roosevelt. In fact, Secret Service protection for Presidents came about because of the McKinley assassination in 1901, which put T.R. into the White House.

Now, however, the exceptionally professional Presidential Protective Detail protects the President of the United States and his family. The Secret Service uses sets of very carefully established procedures to ensure the protection of the President and is run by career professionals who have years of expertise and experience in Secret Service operations.

The current Director of the United States Secret Service, Mark J. Sullivan, began his career as a special agent with the Detroit Field Office back in 1983, giving him 24 years of experience in the job. The previous director was W. Ralph Basham, who had 28 years with the Secret Service. Going back further, Basham's predecessor was Brian L. Stafford, who served for more than 30 years in the Secret Service.

We recommend the establishment of an Electronic Communication Protection Detail, managed under the auspices of the Secret Service.

People with towering expertise have traditionally fulfilled the various missions of the Secret Service. Although their operations have to be flexible with regard to Presidential desires, these professionals have long understood their primary mission is first to protect the President and, only in absence of a risk, to meet the personal and political desires and needs of the President (which must make for some interesting days for those agents).

It should also be noted here that the Hatch Act vanishes when it comes to Presidential protection. Whether the President is out and about making a policy speech or an unabashed political fund-raising speech, the Presidential Protective Detail is active and doing its job.

Sadly, nothing with the professionalism of the Presidential Protective Detail exists for managing White House email. Internal email management is left to the whims of the IT staff currently employed by the sitting administration.

I recommend the establishment of a career Electronic Communication Protection Detail, managed under the auspices of the Secret Service, with the same level of mission-centric attention to detail and professionalism as the Presidential Protective Detail.

And professionalism and domain expertise are important here. Note that the Secret Service has been led by professionals with years of towering experience. This is in stark contrast to FEMA during Hurricane Katrina.

The then director of FEMA, Mike Brown, had previously spent 11 years managing horse trial judges and stewards at the Arabian Horse Association — not exactly towering expertise for the nation's top emergency manager.

Interesting, isn't it, that the guy appointed to protect the President had a heck of a lot more experience protecting the President than the guy appointed to protect the rest of the country had with protecting anything?

If established, the Electronic Communication Protection Detail must also be led by someone with towering expertise in hands-on IT problem solving and security.

I'd rather see a Kevin Mitnick in charge than a Mike Brown. For those of you not familiar with Kevin, he was convicted in the 1990s for hacking into government and private industry computer systems. At one time, he was considered such a threat that he spent time in solitary confinement. The authorities were convinced that if he had access to anything electronic, he might somehow launch nuclear weapons (true story). Today, having served his time, Kevin advises companies on computer security.

The point here is that the Electronic Communication Protection Detail I've proposed must be populated with exceptional IT and security people, not "I know a guy in Tennessee." Like the Presidential Protective Detail, protection of email security must come before the preferences of the protectees. Too much is at stake to blur the line between convenience and protection.

I believe the Secret Service is uniquely qualified to establish this detail because of its dual missions of Presidential protection and computer-based criminal investigation. The Secret Service operates a network of Electronic Crimes Task Forces and Working Groups, so much of the technical expertise to establish an Electronic Communication Protection Detail is already in place.

The mission of the Electronic Communication Protection Detail needs to include the safeguarding of White House email security, the safeguarding and reliable archiving of all messages, and the overall management of email, instant message, cell phone, and BlackBerry communications within the White House staff.

By having one entity providing oversight and operational management across administrations, and by having that entity be one with an excellent track record of protecting the President and the White House, I predict that White House email will be far more secure.

It's worthy of note that I've specifically included management of cell phones and BlackBerry-style handheld PDAs within the mission of the proposed Electronic Communication Protection Detail. Given that these devices are more powerful than many full-sized computers were during the Reagan Administration, there's a huge potential downside risk if these devices are mismanaged.

Since email, computer files in the form of attachments, key contact lists, and so much more are accessible from and stored within these tiny potential nightmares, I believe they need the same careful and integrated oversight that White House email should be getting.

Recommendation: manage political email via the Electronic Communication Protection Detail

Once a candidate wins an election and moves into the White House, all electronic communication, political or otherwise, needs to be managed by the proposed Electronic Communication Protection Detail.

I discussed the reasoning for this earlier, in my Hatch Act recommendation, but we feel it's necessary that the Electronic Communication Protection Detail be clearly tasked with the management of *all* White House email, not just email that's purely government related.

I have absolutely no problem with the Republican National Committee using a firm like SMARTech to manage non-White House email or email for presidential candidates. In fact, my limited research into SMARTech indicated a qualified company that seems to know its stuff.

However, once a candidate becomes President, the game changes. No longer is the candidate transported in his campaign bus, now The President is transported in Marine One and Air Force One.

Likewise, as I've made abundantly clear in my investigation, White House email, political and otherwise, must be managed by a professional, career Electronic Communication Protection Detail.

Recommendation: archiving must be managed professionally

Without a doubt, enterprise-quality archiving servers need to be set up for the management of all White House email. This technology is offered by many companies. It's solid, tested, and used by the very largest of corporations to comply with their own government-mandated record-keeping regulations.

Once again, I recommend the Electronic Communication Protection Detail manage these systems. I also recommend that all email, policy, political, or otherwise, be archived. Remember that archiving doesn't mean disclosing. The practice of archiving is a technical act, while the practice of disclosing is a political or policy act.

The practice of archiving is a technical act, while the practice of disclosing is a political or policy act.

It's up to the policy-makers to determine whether anything from the archives should be disclosed. But it's up to experienced IT professionals to make sure everything's available if disclosure becomes necessary.

Because technology, media, and file formats are changing at breakneck pace, another responsibility of the Electronic Communication Protection Detail with regard to archiving would be the regular updating of archives to new formats. In fact, I recommend that the entire cumulative library of archives be checked and migrated every four years as technology and file formats change.

Recommendation: handhelds need management, tracking, and self-destruct

Given the rigors of the job, it's not surprising that White House staffers are human. People sometimes lose things. Given the long hours and high stress, I'm not surprised that Karl Rove and, likely, other staffers have lost BlackBerry handhelds. In fact, I'd be surprised if they didn't. I lost my phone once.

Given the reality that these are small machines that, when lost, can do a lot of potential damage, I recommend a comprehensive contingency procedure be put into place when such a device is lost or misplaced.

Each staffer issued such a device needs to be trained to notify the Electronic Communication Protection Detail immediately when the device is lost. My recommendations go further though, into the realm of what can be. While every electronic countermeasure can be circumvented given motivation and skill, countermeasures do help.

I recommend that no communication device be issued to White House staffers without two key features: location and destruction.

I recommend that no communication device be issued to White House staffers without two key features: location and destruction.

Companies like TeleNav offer GPS-equipped devices that provide real-time tracking of employees in the field. Devices like the BlackBerry 8800 and BlackBerry 8700 already contain GPS functionality. If a phone were to be lost, the Electronic Communication Protection Detail should be able to query the phone to find out where it is, and then immediately dispatch a recovery team.

One feature not commonly provided on smartphones is a secure erase function. Like the tape that would self-destruct in fifteen seconds in the *Mission Impossible* TV show, phones and handhelds provided to White House staffers should be equipped with a remotely-triggered self-destruct mechanism.

No, I'm not suggesting blue smoke should come out of the device. Instead, I'm recommending that devices like this be outfitted with firmware-level DoD data wipe technology. Conditions like the failure to properly type in a password or the receipt of a special signal sent to the phone would cause the phone to begin a wiping process on all internal data. Obviously, there's no guarantee that a wipe would complete, but this is an added level of security that should exist on all phones used by White House staffers.

While some custom work would be necessary, this is not a hard technology to implement. All that would be necessary are software changes — and a mechanism to make sure the phone doesn't exhibit any outward signs that it's wiping itself. In fact, if it appears that the phone's battery is dead, it will probably buy enough time for the wipe to complete.

Recommendation: restore full function of the Presidential Records Act

My final recommendation actually *is* political, rather than technical. Although not directly an email issue, the conflict between the intent of the Presidential Records Act and the restrictions of Executive Order 12,233 must be resolved.

As I discussed earlier in this book, Executive Order 12,233 virtually guarantees that Presidential records won't be disclosed. Once again, I think it's important to have an informed populace, and I think that by permanently locking presidential records — even from other branches of the government — we lose some of the checks and balances that have proven so essential to America over the years.

Final thoughts

This has been quite the journey down the rabbit hole. What I originally thought was simply a news story about email messages turned out to be an investigation into some potent national security problems. What I thought was a story just about some basic technology turned out to be a wild ride through 25 years of Presidential prerogative.

If you take anything at all away from this book, please make it be this — email in the White House needs to be fixed. Not because we want to give Congress a bigger stick with which to beat on Presidents, but because some really bad things could happen if it's not fixed.

I've included some recommendations in this chapter, but there are still more questions than answers. I've listed many of them during my investigation. Only once all the questions are answered can a more comprehensive policy be defined that will protect our Presidents' ability to conduct business while protecting them from how they conduct business.

In the final chapter, I'll list the questions that have yet to be answered. Go ahead. Turn the page.

Online resources

All of the links in this book are available from the book's Web site. Just visit *EmailsGone.com* and click on the Resources link. That way, you won't have to type in any long URLs.

Read the Hatch Act guidelines at *http://www.osc.gov/ha_fed.htm*.

Learn about TeleNav at *http://www.telenav.com*.

Tips from the ZATZ magazines

When you delete a file from your computer, your camera, or your phone, the data doesn't go away. Instead, a small "deleted flag" is placed with the data. This tells the device that if it needs more storage space, it can use the space used by the deleted file. Until that space is used, though, the file and data remains and can be recovered.

There are some very strong data wiping technologies that can make sure a deleted file can't be recovered. The DoD has developed many such algorithms and you can buy or download software that will DoD wipe your hard drive, your camera's flash card, and, sometimes, your phone's data.

CHAPTER 13

The final questions

As I worked my way through this investigation, I found questions for which I had no answers. Over time, some were answered to a limited extent. For example, one of my early questions asked how many email accounts former Deputy Chief of Staff Karl Rove had while he served in the White House. According to his former assistant, he had three.

But those initial questions were really warm-ups, for as I began my investigation, I had no idea where my research would take me. I thought I was looking for some missing email messages and instead I discovered severe flaws in how the White House handles email — flaws that could result in some terrifying national security consequences.

There are, however, technical issues and concerns, plus security issues and concerns that blast through the political rhetoric and even party affiliation

---

It turns out that the questions about missing email may be more about politics than technology. And, whether we like it or not (and none of us *really* like it), politicians will be politicians. They always have been, and they always will be.

There are, however, technical issues and concerns, plus security issues and concerns that blast through the political rhetoric and even party affiliation. In the previous chapter, I made a series of formal recommendations for how the operational structure of email management in the White House should change.

Over time, my questions got more strident. I found myself becoming more and more worried about the secure transmission of email. My questions got more vehement as I found myself in almost complete disbelief about what appeared to be monumentally inadequate solutions for real problems.

The original article series, this book, and these questions may be of use, not only to our magazines' core audience of technology professionals, but also to members of Congress and IT staff in the White House.

If you're in the latter two categories, please, ask these questions. Seek answers. And fix the problems using some or all of this book's recommendations.

The final questions

I began this book with the question, "Where have all the emails gone?" It seems only fitting that I end this book with the questions that still need good answers.

Question #1: What exact server technology is the Executive Office of the President using?

Question #2: What service is used to transmit White House political and official BlackBerry communications?

Question #3: Did Mr. Rove use more than one BlackBerry?

Question #4: What protocol is used for *GWB43.com* email access?

Question #5: Why would the RNC run so much critical information through a tiny 12-person ISP in Chattanooga?

Question #6: How many White House staffers are just "defaulting" to sending all their email out via their political accounts so that they don't inadvertently slip up and violate the Hatch Act?

Question #7: What, if any, encryption technology is in place to protect important government email sent from political party accounts?

Question #8: Did Mr. Rove and other staffers use Outlook and BlackBerry handhelds for official government business, Republican political business, or both?

Question #9: What email messages are we talking about? Are we talking about email messages sent through the White House *EOP.gov* accounts or the messages sent through the RNC-operated *GWB43.com* accounts?

Question #10: Is the White House operating a separate archive server or are they relying on each individual user to keep track of and/or print out his or her email?

Question #11: Are they stoned?

Question #12: What, did they hire FEMA to come up with their email archiving program? Is Mike Brown the new IT czar at the White House?

Question #13: Did the White House make regular backups?

Question #14: What happened to those backups?

Question #15: What happened to the Domino servers and their hard drives?

Question #16: What happened to all the Notes replications?

Question #17: How is it possible so many messages got lost and no one complained during the migration?

Question #18: If a server blew up and all the past messages were lost, and everybody at the White House knew about it and had to deal with it, how come we haven't heard any "war stories" about the day the email died?

Question #19: So, why, in the middle of a war, did the White House decide to change its email systems?

Question #20: Isn't interrupting such a strategic communications system as email, in the middle of a war, the height of irresponsibility?

Question #21: How could this have happened? Does the White House have any kind of formal policy in place that governs all aspects of email management? If so, what are the details?

Question #22: Were strategic mistakes made because of unreliable email communications at the White House and in the Executive Office of the President before deciding to invade Iraq?

Question #23: Could a crippled email system have led to strategic mistakes in Iraq?

Question #24: If doing this migration at this time wasn't irresponsibility, what was it?

Question #25: Could there have been any benefit to the administration for migrating right in the middle of the prewar buildup?

Question #26: How many BlackBerry devices did Mr. Rove lose?

Question #27: What sort of information was on each BlackBerry when it was lost?

Question #28: What efforts were taken to recover these missing devices and their potentially classified information?

Question #29: If Ms. Ralston is mistaken about Mr. Rove's *ROVE.com* account, could she also be mistaken about other aspects of her testimony?

Question #30: Is Mr. Rove the only one who misplaces these things?

Question #31: Are other key White House staffers losing their communications devices?

Question #32: Just how many times is someone allowed to lose a BlackBerry before being told, "No more"?

Question #33: Has the Hatch Act been used as an excuse to bypass government servers, thereby giving a reasonable-sounding excuse to circumvent the Presidential Records Act and the Federal Records Act?

Question #34: Is IT management at the White House as incomprehensibly unprofessional as it seems — or is a pretense of cluelessness being used to divert questions of disclosure?

Question #35: Where have all the emails gone?

We may never know. But I do know it's not nearly as simple a question as I thought when I began this process.

One final thought... you know what really freaks me out? I've been looking into a very tiny part of Federal government operations and I've discovered some *really* worrisome stuff.

So, here's my final, oh-so-freaky question:

Question #36: Given how big and complex our government is, what else is hidden behind mundane topics and political bluster, that, if brought to light the way I've done with White House email, would send us screaming into the night?

If you take anything at all away from this book, please make it be this — email in the White House needs to be fixed.

Not because we want to give Congress a bigger stick with which to beat on Presidents, but because some really bad things could happen if it's not fixed.

Letters from "Deep Mail"

After I originally published the information from Chapter 5 in *OutlookPower* and *DominoPower* magazines, I got some interesting email from someone with a very anonymous Google Gmail account.

I sent him (or her) back an email, asking for some clarification and specifically asking who he is. The person identified himself as "...one of the researchers with ePluribus Media" and signed his name simply as "Intranets".

This being just too juicy to pass up, we here at ZATZ decided to nickname him "Deep Mail" and publish the information he provided us. Deep Mail continued to send us smaller comments from time-to-time as our coverage continued. You'll need to use your own judgement as to what you think about his comments.

In the meantime, I present to you Deep Mail's first two letters to us. With the exception of some very limited punctuation fixes, the letters are presented to you in a completely unedited form. Keep in mind that I haven't verified any of his claims.

Because of some of the more controversial comments in the letter, I'm obliged to state that the opinions of "Deep Mail" are not necessarily those of the author, the editors, *OutlookPower* or *DominoPower* magazines, ZATZ Publishing, or the Jedi High Council.

Deep Mail's first letter

I appreciate other sources looking into the SMARTech stuff, and have been researching this for over a year. I do question why Microsoft people are doing articles when Averbeck and Mike Connell are so closely tied to Microsoft and have at least some influence (see Averbeck press release on product changes incorporated at their request).

It is also of interest that Connell and GovTech actually worked with Bob Ney to get the House.gov infrastructure moved to Microsoft and privatized committee and Rep's webpages. (House.gov was formerly Unix before GovTech and Ney change over to MS). In your article, you said:

> *"Sadly, our source here is anything but objective. So we can't accept ePluribus' rant as independent information."*

Just for your information, I don't see ePluribus Media as very liberal, many of the posters there are liberal and cross post their blog stuff there, but the foundation is citizen journalism and the folks who have looked into the SMARTech stuff are science types who also stray away from conspiracies.

But the facts are clear that Blackwell did, in fact, contract out the Election Night website to GCR (who subcontracted to New Media/GovTech and SMARTech to host the election night website). The contracts and proof are all in the ePM story, and the SOS office will gladly admit this did take place.

Over on Cannonfire there was a commenter who claims to have sent email to gwb43.com that bounced and the headers had some valuable info, like an intranet IP for a rnc-bes (10.xx.xx.xx) which would imply the RNC is running a Blackberry Enterprise Server out of their IP block in VA. RNC has a block, as well as a DC/VA block for AirNet (same thing as SMARTech) so it's not clear where the "Store and Forward" emails go through which DC address and IP block. I couldn't confirm the bounced emails and never got any myself so I can't confirm the internal rnc-bes server.

In regards to Trespassers-W, Coptix was the primary DNS for all those domains, and in June of 2006, transferred 1600+ domains to smartechcorp.net as primary DNS. Really, there is no direct link from RNC to Coptix, so I'll caution you about your reference to more stuff on trespassers-w.

You should read the Sun article by CTFP which has a quote from Averbeck. The Chattanooga Times Free Press (CTFP) is now owned by Tom Griscom who is Reagan's former Communcations Director and is very friendly to SMARTech, Corker, and Coptix (who redesigned the CTFP webpage) There is a nice quote from Averbeck's wife about the early voting and how she already voted for Corker which the CTFP ran in Oct 2006.

If you want me to fact check anything, or have technical questions, I can steer you in the right direction.

My major concern (aside from the election website) is that all these emails are going through unsecured servers and it is possible Rove or others have sent classified emails or attachments through these uncontrolled, no EOP oversight servers.

(Also of interest is that an ex-GovTech employee now works as WH communications who is quoted about the gwb43 servers...) David Almacy, White House Internet and e-communications director (at http://www.washingtonpost.com/wp-dyn/articles/A4686-2005Apr20.html).

Deep Mail's second letter

I'm one of the researchers with ePluribus Media who has been digging up much of the same online stuff you have recently done.

Coptix still IS the secondary DNS as they used to have a physically off-site DNS server located at a Rackspace NOC. What is interesting is that in the last two weeks they have moved to 1&1 NOC for trespassers-w.net

Jeffrey Cross was mostly a one man operation, and I believe had more technical savvy and provided at least backup DNS, if not all of the DNS for the huge list of clients at ST3 (which eventually became Smartech after the bankruptcy). Cross has more recently brought on more graduates from the local Covenant College (where Cross is a graduate of) to turn Coptix into a graphics/design shop.

(Many of the early WHOIS come back to cross-cc.com Cross Computer Consulting)

We have been tracking domain registrations and got a notice in mid 2006 of transfer from Coptix to Smartech, so maybe you can find some older whois/DNS records in the abuse newsgroups that show tresspassers-w as primary DNS.

I'm not sure it is really that relevant as Coptix was never paid by RNC and mostly just managed DNS in exchange for rack space in the Smartech NOC (and according to Cross, "discounts").

Assuming you can trust the "Jeffrey" that posts to CorrenteWire which I have found no reason not to believe it, that is pretty much the history of recent Coptix adventure into misinformation. (Search Correntewire for "gwb43")

It appears Cross first started posting there, and when no one emailed him or redacted any connection from tresspassers-w to RNC, they cooked up this Rove photo prank. Josiah Roe and Cross make it pretty clear in their posts that the Rove/Coptix photo prank was because people were following the DNS trail, much like you are looking into. When no one took him at his word about the RNC and Coptix, they posted links on many "lefty" blogs about "check out this photo"

Where they photoshopped the Coptix logo into a Rove photo and back edited a blog post from Feb. and edited a second blog post to add more evidence to the photo as having existed since Rove visited Chattanooga.

You can read the CTFP article about the Rove photo. Don't believe anything about April Fools prank, they posted the photo on March 30th and kept up the fake photo until well after April 2nd. They later spun it to a viral marketing campaign, but Cross mentions it was about getting even for poor journalism online.

So, just FYI, Coptix didn't like people looking into their involvement with RNC.

The most I can find on Coptix is the smear website kerry-04.org (go ahead and nslookup w3.coptix.com and check out that webpage) http://www.sourcewatch. org/index.php?title=American_Patriots_Against_John_Kerry

I'd welcome any thing you do find on Trespassers-w, and there is a lot of disinformation, so don't take my word without checking, but I'm afraid I haven't found anything beyond secondary (maybe at one point primary) DNS service.

- *Former TX Rackspace*
- *209.61.172.168   a.ns.trespassers-w.net*
- *209.61.172.169   a.mx.trespassers-w.net*
- *209.61.172.171   pigletmail.mx.coptix.com*
- *New 1&1*
- *82.165.241.22*
- *Reverse: mailer3.coptix.com*
- *Aliases:a.ns.trespassers-w.net*

Thanks,
Intranets (ePM researcher)

My conclusion

So, there you go. Deep Mail checks in. Because I'm insisting on only using independently verifiable sources in this own investigation and always go for an official source when possible, I'm didn't try to verify or expand on Deep Mail's comments. We leave that as an exercise for you, Gentle Reader.

Online resources

All of the links in this book are available from the book's Web site. Just visit *EmailsGone.com* and click on the Resources link. That way, you won't have to type in any long URLs.

To read an article about David Almacy, visit *http://www.washingtonpost.com/wp-dyn/articles/A4686-2005Apr20.html*.

Deep Mail also suggests visiting *http://www.sourcewatch.org/index.php?title=American_Patriots_Against_John_Kerry*.

An interview with Roger Matus on email archiving and retrieval

In *DominoPower Magazine,* we regularly interview experts and technology developers about their companies, products, and strategies. In April 2007, I had the opportunity to interview Roger Matus, CEO and co-founder of InBoxer, Inc.

In this very timely, in-depth interview, Roger helped us understand some of the issues involved in making sure an organization's email is archived and can be found in the event of a legal situation.

David: *Please introduce yourself and tell us about your background.*

Roger: Thank you for inviting me, Dave. I'm the CEO and co-founder of InBoxer, Inc. I've been in software for about 25 years and worked on the development of an email product back in 1983. But I've spent much of the past decade working on speech and language technology in business applications.

David: *I know you come from a speech recognition background. How did you get from speech technology to mail management? Does your experience in speech recognition give you any special skill, perspectives, technology that can be applied to email management?*

Roger: Actually, InBoxer is a marriage of my early software work and speech. Much of InBoxer's proprietary technology is based on classification techniques deployed in speech recognition.

When most people think of speech recognition, they believe the hard problem is to convert sound to a bit pattern. Actually, much of the hard part is deciding what word is meant by what sound. For example, take the sentence "Mr. Wright will write a letter right now." How do you know which wright/write/right is right?

How do you know which wright/write/right is right?

That is where classification techniques are important. To classify a sound, you need to use context and the other words in the sentence or document. Words also have multiple meanings and many words can mean the same thing. To determine intent, you need to use context and other words in the document.

InBoxer does something similar to speech recognition in order to classify a message. That is one of the reasons why InBoxer is much more effective than competitive products. InBoxer classifies and finds messages that keywords cannot. For example, any product may be able to find emails with dirty words, but InBoxer can find potentially harassing email and jokes that do not contain any dirty words.

David: *What exactly is your email appliance?*

Roger: The InBoxer Anti-Risk Appliance is the first rack-mount server for email archiving, search and discovery, and real-time compliance that is easy-to-install and easy-to-use with minimal IT effort. It is typically takes about an hour to install at IBM Lotus Domino sites and helps organizations to quickly meet the needs of the Federal Rules of Civil Procedure.

How does it work? Well, it connects to the Domino journal and copies every email message and attachment. It immediately classifies messages using about 70 tests and creates a full-text index.

The system archives the messages without ever changing the original message. It has a fast, flexible searching and discovery system that can be used by executives, legal counsel, HR professionals, and others can find messages with minimal IT involvement. It also can create real-time alerts and scheduled reports so that the company can monitor ongoing issues.

David: *Doesn't the scanning and archiving of company mail open the organization up to some interesting liabilities? Why is a product like your appliance important to today's large corporation?*

Roger: People used to think that they could protect themselves if they deleted messages instead of archiving them. The logic was that if the message does not exist, it cannot be used as evidence.

The problem is that exact copies of incriminating email do exist. They may be on desktop PCs, printed papers, BlackBerry handhelds, or the email server of an ISP. If there is a chance that anyone at your organization has a copy of an email on their computer, under the newly revised Federal Rules of Civil Procedure, you *must* be able to produce it. Even if it is on an employee laptop in a remote part of the country, you *must* produce it.

Fines for failure to produce emails have been staggering. For example, the largest single sex discrimination verdict in U.S. history, $29.2 million, came after UBS Warburg could not produce copies of relevant emails.

Of course, there is more than one way to produce every relevant email. I've talked to an attorney at a company that had to collect every laptop and hard drive to search for relevant documents. It is expensive and disruptive.

The safest thing to do is to archive messages with a fast retrieval system so that you have a copy and don't need to chase every employee.

David: *How is this device relevant, specifically, to Lotus installations?*

Roger: InBoxer saves IT costs, legal expenses, and reduces the risk of fines and adverse judicial rulings. It is relevant because almost any organization could find itself in a federal court case governed by the FRCP (Federal Rules of Civil Procedure). Examples of federal civil cases include any interstate lawsuit (such as one from an out-of-state customer), any EEOC (Equal Employment Opportunity Commission) case, any immigration case, and any IRS tax case.

InBoxer saves IT costs, legal expenses, and reduces the risk of fines and adverse judicial rulings.

By the way, I read an article today that said that even Canadian firms should follow the U.S. FRCP if they do any business in the U.S.

Of course, Lotus Notes certainly has data management and retrieval capabilities. But, these are not optimized for electronic discovery under the Federal Rules of Civil Procedure. For example, it does not have any process for placing litigation holds on messages to prevent deletion.

InBoxer also finds messages that other systems miss. I often give the example of a "dumb blonde" joke. These jokes may not have a single dirty word, so they may not be found if you do a keyword search. But, these jokes can easily contribute to a hostile work environment.

Another example is that InBoxer has ability to find messages containing any social security number or credit card number to find a privacy leak. Any product can find a specific social security number. But finding any number in a variety of formats is harder.

David: *Compared to most Notes and Domino installations, you're a relatively small company. How can you reassure prospective customers that you're able to maintain this hardware, especially in a worldwide deployment?*

Roger: InBoxer is an IBM Business Partner and a Microsoft Certified Partner. We have provided support to customers on five continents and support some of the largest companies in the world. One Fortune 10 company is an InBoxer customer.

Our hardware support is provided by Dell, which supplies next day on-site hardware support for most of our customers.

David: *So, how much does it cost? what exactly is running inside it? What's the hardware, configuration? What about software? What Linux distro are you running? What other software? What's your code written in?*

Roger: InBoxer starts at $5,000 for the first year for small companies. Our pricing is based on the number of users and is tiered based on required features.

The hardware includes two dual-core Xeon processors, up to 4 gigabytes of RAM, and up to 3 terabytes of internal storage. The total amount of usable archiving storage is virtually unlimited because the system supports networked file servers and low-cost USB drives.

The system runs on an open-source version of Red Hat Linux. InBoxer software is written primarily in Python.

David: *Why sell a box and not simply a software product?*

Roger: Any software product that runs on a Lotus Domino server increases the risk to mission-critical applications. They also require significant IT effort to install, optimize, and manage.

The InBoxer Anti-Risk Appliance is designed to minimize the risk to your operation. It requires minimal IT effort. The InBoxer system arrives pre-configured and is typically installed in less than an hour of IT effort. By the time you have logged in, the system has already started processing mail.

David: *Here at ZATZ, we have enormous email archives and email flow, and we're also a relatively tiny company. How can you be sure to provide enough disk space to archive all the flow from the large companies and installations that typically deploy Domino?*

Roger: The InBoxer Anti-Risk Appliance supports virtually unlimited archival storage. In addition to the up to 3 terabytes of internal storage, the system gives you a lot of choices.

Do you already backup your systems? If so, InBoxer can compress and archive messages to your networked file storage system. Your existing backup procedures can handle the rest. There is no need to create a redundant storage system.

Don't have a back-up system? InBoxer can archive to low cost USB drives. I saw a 1TB USB hard drive online yesterday for $350. That is easy to add.

If you want to go off-site, InBoxer also supports off-site storage hosted by *Amazon.com*.

We are able to use expandable storage with the Federal Rules of Civil Procedure.

First, to make sure that archived files are not changed, InBoxer creates an encrypted signature for each file. The archived file signature must match the record kept by InBoxer to prove authenticity. This step helps you in your efforts to establish the chain of custody of a message.

Second, no matter what you choose, InBoxer will keep a local copy of any message placed on "litigation hold" to prevent accidental deletion of a message that must be kept.

David: *How does your offering compete against, say, Postini? How about AXS-One, who we've interviewed before?*

Roger: Dave, I will never say a bad word about a competitor. Both Postini and AXS-One are successful companies with loyal customers. We position ourselves differently.

The InBoxer Anti-Risk Appliance is the only product that provides archiving, electronic discovery, and real-time compliance alerts in an easy-to-install and easy-to-use appliance.

I suggest that Domino sites look at everyone. Even if you decide not to select InBoxer, I can tell you some things to look for.

Make sure that whatever product you pick will capture every email message, including internal mail. Internal email is critical because it contains most of the off-the-cuff, casual email conversations that tend to trigger lawsuits and arm litigators with evidence. This is a good question to ask hosted solutions vendors because many require extra services to configure systems for internal mail.

Make sure that your product never changes the original email or you risk spoiling the evidence. You may be surprised to learn that some well established solutions add metadata or otherwise change messages.

Ask about how easy is it to find emails you need. I have a couple of questions you can ask. How easy is it to find offensive messages that do not contain dirty words? Can your system distinguish between emails that mention a competitor's product and an email addressed to a competitor? Can you find any message that contains any credit card number?

Can you protect messages from being deleted accidentally or intentionally? Violations of "litigation hold" provisions can lead to significant penalties or adverse judgments.

Can you create accounts for your HR executive and legal counsel? Or, will requests require IT help?

And, can you monitor for on-going problems? For example, it is not enough just to find harassing email. You need to know whether the harassment has stopped or your company could face penalties.

David: *What else should we know?*

We really care about IBM Lotus Domino and worked hard to implement InBoxer correctly. While some companies may claim that they work with Domino, many of them don't understand the problems or require professional services.

InBoxer worked with IBM employees in IBM facilities to make sure that the InBoxer Anti-Risk Appliance will work well in IBM Lotus Domino environments. I am happy to say that the InBoxer Anti-Risk Appliance has been awarded the "Ready for IBM Lotus Domino software" emblem from IBM as the result of the effort.

For those in a mixed shop, it is worth mentioning that the product is exactly the same product as the one for Microsoft Exchange. So, if you have Domino in some locations and Exchange in others, the same InBoxer unit can handle both and create a common email archive.

Online resources

All of the links in this book are available from the book's Web site. Just visit *EmailsGone.com* and click on the Resources link. That way, you won't have to type in any long URLs.

For more information on InBoxer, visit *http://www.inboxer.com*.

Tips from the ZATZ magazines

Both Lotus Notes and Microsoft Outlook provide user-level archiving functions. These are designed to free up space within a user's mail database file.

There's nothing wrong with allowing users to archive their own mail. Backing up and archiving are activities that all computer users should practice.

However, there also needs to be an enterprise-level archiving strategy that stores email away for future reference and that can't be deleted by users.

What your company can learn from the White House email problem

BY ROGER MATUS

What will you do when the White House email problem becomes your email problem? The current uproar about email retention at the White House may have direct meaning for Notes/Domino and Exchange sites. There are really two issues: how long is your retention policy and which email messages are exempt from retention?

Current coverage of the problem

Let's review some of the facts of the current White House email problem:

- From 2001 to 2004, the Republican National Committee had an email retention policy of 30 days, according to a letter written by Rep. Henry Waxman (D-CA), chairman of the House Committee on Oversight and Government Reform, on April 12.

- At least 88 White House staffers have official as well as political email addresses that were provided by the Republican National Committee, according to *The Washington Post*. Email domains used by the staffers include *GWB43.com, GEORGEWBUSH.com,* and *RNCHQ.org.*

- Millions of official White House email messages may be missing, White House spokeswoman Dana Perino acknowledged. "I wouldn't rule out that there were a potential five million emails lost," she said.

There was nothing illegal about the length of the RNC's email retention policy for RNC mail. An argument can be made that the deletion of certain official correspondence violates the Presidential Records Act.

If true, the issue would not have been the RNC retention policy for RNC mail. It would have been if official correspondence was knowingly placed on RNC systems to avoid the White House archiving system or if RNC officials knew that official correspondence was being deleted.

In the same way, in the absence of specific regulatory obligations, such as those for certain financial institution transactions, organizations can create any retention policy they wish. Even the new Federal Rules of Civil Procedure (FRCP) do not mandate a specific archiving policy. They just say that if a copy exists anywhere within an organization, the copy must be found in a specified timely manner. If you're concerned about this for your organization, contact your legal counsel.

It turns out that it is simply easier for most organizations to archive every email message because it is much easier to retrieve them from a centralized location. Some companies have complied with discovery requests by collecting the hard drives from every personal computer to search for copies of email messages. That works too.

The more interesting question for IT may relate to the 88 or so White House staffers that have political email addresses.

Issues of apparent authority

It is often recommended that companies allow individuals to use non-company operated email accounts for personal mail.

Web-based email services like Google's Gmail, Microsoft's MSN Mail, and Yahoo! Mail allow employees to conduct private matters without involving the business. For example, there is no reason why a company should know about an individual's family matters, personal habits, medical appointments, or financial affairs.

Even further is the legal concept of "apparent authority." An email message that comes from your organization's domain may appear to be written on behalf of the organization. A person who would never think of writing a letter on corporate letterhead to a financial institution for a personal matter might not even think twice about using a corporate email account for the same content.

The 88 or so White House staffers may have had excellent reasons for keeping political mail separate from official government mail because of "apparent authority." For example, it is more appropriate for a partisan email to come from *RNCHQ.org* than *WhiteHouse.gov* or *EOP.gov.* An interpretation of the Hatch Act would suggest that partisan use of government systems is also illegal.

The problem comes when official mail is sent from a personal email account. What happens when those messages are not part of the corporate archive? In the case of the White House staffers, the appearance is not great. Here are some excerpts from email messages that were not in the White House system:

- "I now have an RNC blackberry which you can use to email me any time. No security issues like my WH (White House) email," wrote Susan Ralston, Karl Rove's former executive assistant, to two lobbyists working for Rove on July 11, 2001.

- "...I can access my AOL email when necessary so if you need to send me something that I need to read, you can send to my AOL email and then call and page me to check," wrote Ralston to Jack Abramoff himself.

Of course, the White House employees have the requirements of the Presidential Records Act of 1978, which states that all Presidential records belong to the United States government. If government records were destroyed intentionally, additional problems may arise.

For other organizations, the appearance of bypassing corporate archiving systems may cause a problem in the court of public opinion, if not a court of law. The problem is compounded if such email messages become public, like the two excerpts displayed above, before corporate IT and legal are aware of them. Remember that email messages may never be truly lost when you remember that while a sender may delete an email, the receiver also has a copy.

What's a company to do?

A company must first decide whether to allow the personal use of corporate systems. While this is not an alternative for partisan email on White House systems due to the Hatch Act, it is a safe approach from an archival perspective. Every message is kept. The downside is the additional resources required for personal mail and the "apparent authority" of corporate systems.

Techniques need to be used to limit "apparent authority" with personal use of corporate systems. A disclaimer could be required for personal mail. Or, conversely, a disclaimer could be mandatory except when the employee designates that it is business mail. This would require companies publish and train users on the definition of business mail, as well as acceptable use policies. Of course, with the Hatch Act, partisan use of White House computers would probably not be a good idea.

A company must also decide whether to permit the use of Web-based or other personal email systems. The problem is that there is no way to prevent employees from using such systems for business mail. Language based filters to detect personal mail, such as the one from my company, InBoxer, are good — but far from perfect. For example, is it personal or business mail to invite a neighbor, who may become a customer, to a baseball game?

Whatever is decided, be prepared to enforce it uniformly. In a recent Virginia case, a newspaper had a policy that prohibited personal use of corporate email system. According to the case (Richmond Times Dispatch v National Labor Relations Board, March 15, 2007), it was first enforced when employees were organizing a union. Selective enforcement was not allowed.

Roger Matus is an expert on email archiving and retrieval. He is the CEO and co-founder of InBoxer, Inc., has been in the software business for about 25 years, and worked on the development of an email product back in 1983. He's spent much of the past decade working on speech and language technology in business applications and has recently begun to use his language technology to create a smart email archiving system.

Tips from the ZATZ magazines

If you use a Web-based email service, you often don't need to run any special email client program (like Notes or Outlook) on your computer.

Instead, you connect to the service via your Web browser. The email is stored on the provider's computers and you can generally access all your email from anywhere.

Web-based email is usually free, paid for by advertisers who display their ads while you read your email.

An interview with Marie Patterson on email storage and retrieval

In April 2006, I had the opportunity to interview Marie Patterson. Marie's a Vice President of AXS-One, a company that specializes in records management and compliance.

While the topic of email storage and retrieval at first seems incredibly dry, once you read this interview, you'll be shocked at what could happen if you don't have good email storage and retrieval procedures in place.

David: *Please introduce yourself and tell us what you do for AXS-One. What's your background personally?*

Marie: I'm the Vice President for Corporate Marketing. I've worked in the software industry for almost 20 years, primarily in the area of archiving and archiving-based software solutions for the past 10.

David: *Why is email archiving, storage, and retrieval an important issue for network managers and C-level executives to care about?*

Marie: While organizations have accelerated their use of email to the point that the majority of all communication and transactions are now conducted via email, it would appear that only a minority have really thought through the effects of that decision — either from an IT or business perspective. As a result, companies face exponentially growing infrastructure costs. So while the actual cost of storage has decreased, companies are still stuck with the overhead of that increased storage, increased backups, management, etc.

At the C-level, the real issue is again the lack of policies, as we're seeing in much-publicized cases like Morgan Stanley. Executives are concerned about anything that will affect shareholder value.

As it relates to email, the issues are all risk related, so growing and un-budgeted e-discovery costs definitely affect the bottom line. Litigation that has to go to settlement because organizations are incapable of finding specific records affect the bottom line.

High-profile litigation that ends up on the front page of the Wall Street Journal makes the organization look either incompetent or fraudulent. That affects the corporate image which, again, affects shareholder value.

David: *On your Web site, you talk about records compliance management. Please explain why this is important for large companies.*

Marie: Growing volumes of electronic records are a fact of life for every organization. Add to that the 10,000+ regulations around the world that dictate retention, management, or privacy of those records, plus growing issues regarding litigation.

As a result, we believe that within the next 3-5 years, every organization worldwide will need software assistance to enable them to manage their electronic records — for operational reasons, to comply with regulations, to facilitate legal discovery as well as for broad risk management and mitigation reasons.

David: *It sounds like your business is aimed at, well, helping businesses protect themselves from horror stories. Can you tell us a few horror stories to help us get some perspective on why this is such a concern?*

Marie: Remember, this issue affects organizations of pretty much any size in every market sector worldwide. However, there are a few that have been heavily publicized in the past year. Let's start with the ongoing saga at Morgan Stanley.

Last year [2005] the company made headlines after being slapped with a multi-billion dollar judgment due, in part, to its inability to certify that it had turned over all relevant emails to the plaintiffs' lawyer. The judge in the case, frustrated at Morgan Stanley's repeated failure to comply with the discovery order, handed down a pre-trial ruling that effectively found the bank had conspired to "defraud" its former client.

And there's the now-infamous UBS Warburg v. Zubulake case, in which UBS was ordered to pay Laura Zubulake $29.2 million in damages in a sexual discrimination case that involved destroyed or non-discoverable email.

And proving that this issue isn't limited to the commercial sector, in the current investigation of former White House staffer Lewis Libby, there are problems over the issue that certain emails can't be located.

David: *We often hear people talking about the cost of storage, but isn't that old news? With a terabyte of storage costing less than a thousand dollars, isn't storage incredibly cheap?*

Marie: Absolutely — the price of storage has definitely come down and that's great news for users. But the issue here isn't storage, and just having a backup strategy wouldn't be enough to prevent some of the horror stories alluded to earlier. This issue has far more to do with the risk that the content contained in the storage devices generates. And even for organizations that believe they're not really affected by legislation or litigation, more storage means more overhead, which means longer backup cycles, which means more people.

There's also an additional point to consider: the content is stored for a reason, or a lot of reasons — compliance, corporate governance, legal discovery, operational support, knowledge management, etc., and that content therefore needs to be completely and truly accessible.

As those headline-making cases have shown, storage just is not the complete solution.

David: *Notes has excellent data management and retrieval. How do you add value over the basic Notes offering?*

Marie: The Notes environment certainly has data management and retrieval capabilities, but these don't provide a solution for organizations looking to reduce costs associated with growing volumes of Notes email.

That's where functionality such as Single Instance Storage comes into its own. We have comprehensive mailbox management capabilities, such as "soft" quotas to automatically manage mailbox sizes and support for offline/laptop users.

We have extensive retention and records management capabilities, which is really important for organizations that need to retain email for compliance reasons, for instance. Plus, we enable organizations to capture all email — inbound, outbound and internal (and then set retention on it).

So regardless of what users decide to do once they receive an email, alter it, delete it, etc., the organization can be confident that it has an irrefutable copy of email records. Generally speaking, you don't want your end users being one man/woman records managers and deciding what's important and therefore needs to be retained.

> **Generally speaking, you don't want your end users being one man/woman records managers and deciding what's important and therefore needs to be retained.**

As we archive email, we full text index it (as well as any attachments), to ensure that you can find it in the future. And with the information archived, we offer a lot of "value add" functionality, such as the ability to set retention periods and suspend normal retention in the event of litigation case holds.

We have the concept of "active case management" that's really valuable during e-discovery processes. We've developed patent pending search capabilities that provide Google-like search speeds as well as a search interface (the Search Wizard) to make the search process very simple for non-IT users (who are increasingly involved in the e-discovery process).

Another key function is process chain of custody. We retain an auditable log of every email we archive, which is essential if you want to prove that the email we've archived is an irrefutable copy.

And finally, our Lotus Notes capabilities are part of a single archiving and records management platform for any electronic record. This is crucial as organizations start to develop and enforce policies around all electronic records, rather than silo'd archiving solutions.

David: *Even though storage is cheap, I'd imagine finding a single email message in a 50 terabyte storage array might be quite a challenge. What's your technology and how does it help in this situation?*

Marie: That's exactly the thought on most network managers' minds right now — even if the content is all there, how long will it take to search through it? We're aware that this is starting to become a big issue for a number of vendors in this market — they can get the stuff into the archive, but finding it quickly and accurately is a whole different issue.

We've been in the archiving market for 13 years, so we're used to working with customers that have massive volumes of records archived. Last year we took search capabilities to another level when we announced patent-pending technology, called Rapid-AXS, as an integrated part of our solution. It uses grid architecture and commodity hardware to radically improve foreground search speeds. For instance, it takes searches that maybe took 20 minutes down to seconds.

David: *Do you see email declining over the next few years with threats from spam, spyware, and other malware attacks? What's the real level of email use in business.*

Marie: Not a chance — impossible as it seems, the volume of email is going to keep going up. The Radicati Group says that the email client base will increase from 1.9 billion seats in 2006 to nearly 3.6 billion seats in 2010, representing an average annual growth rate of 18%. Over the next seven years, it's been estimated that a company with 20,000 employees will have to save approximately 4.5 billion emails.

Imagine the complexity involved in just ensuring that the right emails are retained for the right period of time. Now imagine searching through all that archived content if there's an audit, legal discovery order or similar request.

For the record, the ePolicy Institute reports the following scary statistics:

- 21% of employee email is subpoenaed by courts and regulators.

- 13% of companies have battled lawsuits triggered by employee email.

- 65% of companies lack email retention policies.

- 94% of companies fail to retain and archive instant messages.

- 46% of companies offer employees no email policy training.

- 50% of workplace instant messages users send or receive is risky content including attachments, jokes, gossip, confidential info, and porn.

David: *Who are your competitors? Don't IBM and Legato offer similar solutions? How are you different?*

Marie: There are other vendors in this market. However, most entered this space to address operational issues, as in, "How do I reduce the size of users' mailboxes?" That requires a fundamentally different approach to archiving in order to retain irrefutable copies of email for regulatory or governance issues. So our technology went out of the door from Day 1 to address not just operational issues but also compliance and governance. This meant that from Day 1, our solution addressed scalability, performance, records management, chain of custody, litigation support, etc.

David: *You see business communication en-masse. What does the future hold for business communication in five years and ten years? Will we see more or less of email? Will there be issues of tracking IMs, VOIP, and other technologies?*

Marie: In the near term one big issue will be instant messaging. There's an entire generation now entering the workplace that communicates constantly through IM, yet most of it is never archived or even captured. And since people might feel more comfortable in this medium, the content is more frank, which makes it ripe for e-discovery. On the flip side, companies have trouble complying with such e-discovery because they don't capture the content.

Looking forward, it's possible to envision a kind of business where every kind of business communication — phone calls, workplace audio-video, keystrokes — is captured, digitized and archived. And it could all end up in court.

Online resources

All of the links in this book are available from the book's Web site. Just visit *EmailsGone.com* and click on the Resources link. That way, you won't have to type in any long URLs.

For more information on AXS-One, visit *http://www.axsone.com.*

INDEX